Theatre The

Michael Bogdanov is a theatre director of inte...
He has directed Shakespeare in many of the world's leading
theatres and with major theatre companies including the Royal
Shakespeare Company. He was Associate Director of the
Royal National Theatre for eight years and he co-founded the
English Shakespeare Company in 1986 with actor Michael
Pennington. He was also Chief Executive of the Deutsches
Schauspielhaus (National Theatre) in Hamburg, 1989–1992.
He has won numerous awards at home and abroad including
the Society of West End Theatres (SWET) Best Director for
his production of *The Taming of the Shrew* (RSC) and the
Laurence Olivier Award for Best Director for his seven-play
history cycle *The Wars of the Roses* (ESC). He lives in Cardiff
and Hamburg.

Capercaillie Books

Theatre
The Directors Cue

Thoughts and Reminiscences

Michael Bogdanov

Capercaillie Books

First published by Capercaillie Books Limited in 2013.

Registered office 1 Rutland Court, Edinburgh

© Michael Bogdanov. The moral rights of the author have been asserted.

Printed by Antony Rowe, Chippenham

Set in Galliard by 3btype.com, Edinburgh

A catalogue record of this book is available from the British Library.

ISBN 978-1-909305-34-2

To Gottfried Greiffenhagen.
In memory of the many inspiring conversations.

Dipping into my memory bank has been somewhat akin to blindly pinning the tail on the donkey, or thrusting a hand into the bran tub to see what emerges. There are, I realise, still lots of bits and pieces of all shapes and sizes – the good, the bad and the x-factor – nestling in the sawdust waiting to be plucked out. And if there is sometimes a tendency to indulge in a bit of granny egg sucking it is because I hope a few people not in the know will find what directors do mildly interesting. I have – for fifty years.

Michael Bogdanov, April 2013.

Contents

1

What's In a Name

My real name is Bogdin. It's a nice short little Ukrainian name and I once had the distinction of being the only Bogdin in the phone book in the whole of Great Britain. I spent ten hours one day in the British Museum Library when I was twelve, checking. It means 'son of' or 'who is of God'. So does Michael. An example of two positives making a negative.

Bogdin. B-O-G-D-I-N. Simple you would think to pronounce and write. Nog a bin of id. Bigdin, Bodgin, Badgin, Bigbin, Bogpan, Dogbin, Dodgin, Bogpen, Biggie, Boggie, Baggie – whatever variant you come up with, I've had it. The crunch came when I received a cheque from the Irish Times for an article I had written for 1s 11d (you can tell how long ago that was) made out to M. Bogie. I thought – right, that's it – and I changed my name to the professional one of Bogdanov, the surname of a Polish cousin ten times removed. If you want something to mess up, try that. At least it would make people concentrate.

For a time, it all worked wondrously. Apart from the 'V' turning into a 'U' an 'R' or an 'FF', it had the effect of focusing the collective dyslexia perfectly. Until computers got hold of it. Computer error, Sir. There's nothing wrong with my tipping.

Then suddenly the whole name game collapsed around my ears in one go. I was giving a lecture at the University of Florida, Talahassee, and the Professor of the Drama Faculty introduced me.

(Imagine a deep Southern drawl). 'I'd now like y'all to welcome he-yar one of the world's great theatre directors. Put your hands together and welcome all the way from London, England – Mr Michael Dogbananas!' I laughed. 'Would that it were so' I said, 'but my name is Bogdanov'. Face aghast! 'Gaard, I'm really, really sorry! Look, Mr Darnoff, may I call you Bob?' Q.E.D. That and Bogdoornob. A teacher at Howells School, Llandaff, where I had been giving a talk. To the eight year olds. – 'Thank Mr Bogdoornob nicely'. Chorus of eight year olds – 'Thank you Mr Bogdoornob'.

If you must choose a name other than your own to operate under professionally, make sure to choose one that cannot be confused with anyone else working in an associated field. I suspect that Bogdin, had I been able to live patiently with the corruption, would not have wrought confusion. As it was, through the 70's, when I was working at the Newcastle Playhouse, phone calls mixed me up with the then Newcastle and England footballer – hushed voice on the end of the line, mishearing – 'Mum, it's Malcolm MacDonald!' MacDonald is still common. ('Aye, Madam, 'tis common' – Hamlet).

But the worst is having that little known film director Peter Bogdanovich hanging around my neck. Even good friends sometimes inadvertently address me as my namesake. Christopher Morahan, an Associate with me at the Royal National Theatre, congratulating me on my SWET (Society of West End Theatres) Director of the Year Award – 'Well done, Peter'. Tom Kempinski, playwright, pens a letter – 'Dear Peter, this is an offer of employment . . .'. Young actor hopefuls write for jobs – Dear Mr Bogdanovich, Dear Peter Bogdanov. So it didn't surprise me, as a result of an essay that I wrote for *The New Statesman*, castigating critics for their ignorance and inaccuracy, that Peter Popham of *The Independent* should retaliate with a blistering attack on the wrong man.

I was once standing in the foyer of the Phoenix Theatre, Leicester, a Young People's and Community theatre, seating 250 people of which I was the Artistic Director. It was Christmas 1977. The first night had just taken place of my version of *Dracula*, an adult participation fun show. The audience post-show *Dracula* feast was in full swing on stage – Garlic Sausage, Gingerbread crosses, Bulls Blood wine etc. A man came up to me, collar and tie.

'Mr Bogdanovich?'

'Yes'.

'Jolly good show'.

'Thank you'.

'However there is one thing I've been meaning to say to you for some time. I think you got the end of *The Last Picture Show* wrong. You know the shot where . . .' I interposed:

'Wait a minute, don't you mean Peter Bogdanovich?'

'Yes, that's you isn't it?'

I laughed. 'Somehow, I don't think that Peter Bogdanovich would be standing in the foyer of the Phoenix Theatre Leicester, having directed Dracula for Christmas. However, if you were to try Michael Bogdanov on Sunset Boulevard (a fair swap I thought) he might be able to help you'.

I take comfort from the fact that Peter B. suffers a certain amount of irritation when people at the Oscar ceremonies address him as Mike, or belt up to him in Bel-Air panting 'Michael, I've been looking for you everywhere'. It did happen once. A columnist and writer in L.A., a close friend from Trinity College, Dublin, (and an even closer friend of other stars . . .) received a call from both Pete and Mike on the same day. Confusing the numbers on her message sheet, she rang Peter Bogdanovich and when a sleepy voice answered said 'Michael, this is Bridget'. One back.

This identity crisis finally reached its apotheosis at the time of the tit for tat (awful expression) expulsion of the twelve Russian diplomats in 1987. For some time I had been receiving letters, forwarded from BBC Radio 4, addressed to 'Michael Bogdanov'. So far so good. They began 'I enjoyed your lecture last night on the Kurdistan economy . . .' and 'I found your dissertation on the development of the Russian tractor fascinating. . . .' I thought that someone was playing a practical joke on me and sent them back 'Not Known At This Address'.

One day I received a thick package with a mass of diagrams and plans. Not another bloody tractor! And I threw it in the fire. Then came the expulsions. I turned over the back page of *The Guardian* and there was a picture of a man on the steps of a plane – the Russian diplomat, Michael Bogdanov, who had been here for a year to give a series of lectures for Radio 4 on the Soviet economy. Being expelled.

'At one point' he said 'I became confused with the theatre director of the same name. He even received my mail including a series of plans for a nuclear site in the Highlands of Scotland'.

The phone rang all next day, asking me what I had done to get thrown out. There are many things that might qualify but bullshitting about Russian tractors is not one of them. Theatre possibly.

Get yourself a good name.

2

What is a Director?

What is a director? Part teacher, psychologist, psychiatrist, psycho-analyst, nursemaid, confidant, therapist, elocutionist, gymnast, choreographer, clown, raconteur, poet, painter, architect, writer, editor, child, adult, politician, revolutionary, mediator, trouble-shooter, terrorist. A train driver, a brake man. Street-fighting man, tome-toting pedant. An upholder of tradition, an iconoclastic destroyer. The purveyor of truth, the harbinger of lies. A believer in the power of theatre in whatever form, and wherever it is performed, to change the world.

And many more things.

I confess at some point to having been all of these, on occasions the whole lot in the course of a single day. At such times I believe we earn our money. It's a bastard of a profession.

I am often asked how I would describe myself as a director and I generally evade the question, leaving it to others to provide a variety of (usually disparaging) epithets. I have been called variously – an iconoclast, third-rate, a genius. I should have been – strangled at birth, run out of town, never let near a stage; that radical organ 'The Daily Telegraph' has called me 'a national treasure'. I have been described as – insouciant, irreverent, eccentric; authentic, accomplished, inept; pioneering, Marxist, provocative; conservative, original, incompetent, masterly; (un)disciplined, brash, astonishing; unique, unsubtle, surprising, predictable;

outrageous, life-enhancing, arrogant, exciting, boorish, a buffoon, a joy; and – on the occasion of receiving an Honorary Fellowship from the Royal Welsh College of Music and Drama – 'the most idiosyncratic director at work today'. On my gravestone I would like the word – 'Tried.'

However, if pushed to parade my ego, I could see myself as something like Augusto Boal out of Ken Campbell/ Meyerhold and Littlewood, with a touch of the Compton sweep, the Baylis mission and Nye Bevan's passion thrown in. There's also something of Eric and Ernie out of Tati there too, with a side-step like Barry John. (You can tell my age by the cultural references.) I have had a number of influences – Sartre, Camus, Kerouac when young, Nietzsche, Foucault, Marx when older. No unreconstructed socialist me – just a socialist.

In the theatre, The Living Theatre were a revelation, Brook a confirmation, Jan Kott a consummation, English critics an abomination. I have never consciously tried to imitate or steal anybody's work unless there was an idea that I thought humbly I could develop better in some way. Ideas are a thousand a penny. Nobody has copyright on ideas, least of all directors, and if somebody takes something of mine I wish them well. It only hurts when they use it badly. Later I will name names

I have had a number of heroes and mentors over the years, some more unlikely than others. From left to right; H B Craig, an Irishman who only lasted two terms at my school, the Lower School of John Lyon, Harrow, whose IVth form English lessons consisted solely of letting groups of us compete against each other with improvised playlets. That's why he only lasted two terms. My group was the Boganshosles, a combination of syllables culled from three members – John Walsh, Philip Mansley and myself.

R.B.D. French, grandson of Percy French, Ireland's great tunesmith ('Are you right there, Michael, are you right?'), my tutor and the Chairman of Players, the theatre group at Trinity

College Dublin, who handed over the writing of the Annual Summer Revue after thirty years in the saddle, to myself and Terry Brady. An indelible memory: his vast, ice cold, crumbling Georgian pile of decay and splendour in the Wicklow mountains in the snow. His ninety-five-year old Mother in bed with gloves, black hat and a bottle of Guinness. Six sausages for tea. He ate three, I two. In his overcoat. He offered me the last one. As I reached for it, it was nimbly speared and porked whole with ne'er an upward glance from a book propped up against a bottle of stout. Timing.

Tom McGrath, Irish/Canadian, lugubrious Head of Light Entertainment at Radio Telefis Eireann, Dublin, where as Producer/Director I worked on over one hundred and twenty five programmes in the space of two years. Religion and Gaelic football, Outside Broadcast dramas up mountains in the West of Ireland, travelling news documentaries. Tom hired me straight from a BBC Producers' course: two days later I was in the box directing an hour long weekly live *Show Band* show, 'One Night Stand'. A furnace of a baptism. Tom would say of tricky number 'Kick it, head – if it won't sing it won't work'. I knew what he meant even if nobody else did.

Peter Stevens, administrator of the Nottingham Playhouse with John Neville, opener of new theatres extraordinaire – Newcastle, the Leicester Haymarket, and the (Royal) National Theatre. He took me with him to all of them – artistic directors willing. He said to me, fingers stabbing out, eyes bulging, during a particul-arly bolshie interchange in the foyer of the Newcastle Playhouse 'You're one of the best – but you're trouble'. (I had encouraged Tony Vogel as Caliban in *The Tempest*, totally naked, covered in mud, to go into the foyer in the interval and have a pint. 'Hi day – freedom', I quoted from the play, trying to explain).

Peter Hall, not for standing by, in front and behind, during *The Romans in Britain* affair, but for teaching me a lesson; in theatre – never say never. 'But you said he's a terrible actor' I exploded over Michael Pennington, who a year previously had been denied me as Astrov in *Uncle Vanya* and who Peter was now casting in lead roles in Shakespeare's late plays. Eyes widening, cigar out of mouth, blandly – 'I've changed my mind'. He really should play Claudius.

Victor Glynn, fast talking Mr Fixit, erstwhile head of Golden Square Pictures and Portman Films, but in my days at the Young Vic, press officer. The first Board member of the English Shakespeare Company and still there fourteen years later at the finish. Got *Hiawatha*, my series *Shakespeare Lives* and twenty-four hours of the ESC's *The Wars of the Roses* onto the screen.

Bill Wallis, rotund actor, and Chris Dyer, bearded designer (that is not all I have to say about them), alongside whom at differing periods, I developed, in theory and in practice, my ideas on Shakespeare. Some would say they should be run out of town.

Peter Zadek, for giving me two of the greatest experiences I have ever had in the theatre – *Ghetto* and *Lulu* – thus inspiring me to go and work in Germany. If that's what you can do here, I thought, I want in.

And finally my partner, actor Michael Pennington, with whom I co-founded the English Shakespeare Company, who for ten years fought the system alongside me at the ESC, travelled fifty thousand miles, playing exotically split weeks in Hull/Paris and Blackpool/Karachi and who only once lost his temper – not with the Arts Council, surprisingly, but over the vexed question at the Chicago World Theatre Festival of the unprovided breakfast sausage post 9.00 a.m., without which, it would seem, the Company could not perform. Or get out of bed in time.

Bless.

3

Why Theatre?

Two planks and a passion.

The first plank the stage, the second the ideology on which to build the passion. The passion is to spread that ideology. All art is political. It is protest. At its highest point it is a powerful instrument of social change. The position of theatre within society, makes it ideally placed to aid that change and we, the artists, the theatre practitioners, have a duty to fulfil our elected role as purveyors and vendors of truth as we see it. This can change daily and the theatre responds accordingly, altering its perspective. Why not television and film? I want the live contact of an audience. I want to feel an instant response to what I say. I want an audience to stand up and be counted. To shout *Yes*, to shout *No*, to cheer, to boo, to laugh, to cry, to walk out, to fight, to argue – anything to indicate that what has happened during a performance has moved that audience to feel something and motivated them to do something about that feeling. Arseholes to Aristotle. Boo to Brecht. I want passion and engagement, not catharsis and *verfremdung* (alienation).

Two people meet. One tells a story. Then that same person tells the story again and again and again, each time varying the delivery and each time receiving a different response. One day he or she tells it to one person, the next day to a thousand. There are some people to whom it is told who think up suggestions about how it can be changed. Maybe four or five people can tell it better. Or a thousand. The story changes. Each person, each generation, each century adapts it to particular circumstances. Some use costumes to illustrate it, others use settings. Some illustrate it literally, others use fantasy and imagination. Some use images, some use technology. The core of the story has remained the same but around it peoples and cultures have woven a fabric of artifice and artistry, colour and magic, movement and words, light and sound. And it has remained an uniquely live experience, happening only at one moment in time, conferring on the group of people telling and the group listening a very special status. They, and only they at that moment and in that place, are participating, whether in a basement in Brixton, a quarry in Avignon, a dustbowl in Africa or a stadium in Sydney. Or, even in that strange place of reverential worship with the misnomer 'theatre'. They are the privileged ones sharing that communal experience. That's theatre.

And yet it is something much, much more. If theatre were merely the expression of fantasy it would only paint abstract pictures with words; but words and sounds combine to communicate a story. The king is dead – the child is sleeping – the boy is hungry. As we become more sophisticated, so we need to express feelings about ourselves, about society, the world. Words by extension become debate and theatre becomes a debating platform, the natural outlet for all the hopes, wishes, anger, despairs of a community. It becomes that instrument of social change. There are some still telling the original story. There are others now who have turned the story into a moral fable. Some others still want a change of leader and are using the story as an illustration. Theatre is being put to the service of the community. Some stay with Aristotle's version of the story in this debate about leadership, purging their emotions through guilt and through catharsis. Others follow Brecht and calmly debate the possibility of change. Another group over in the corner has collectively decided that the story needs a real ending and have gone out into the streets to gather support for a deposition. There's another group who have set the whole thing to music, as the way to interest people in the subject. There is an excitement in the air. The Story has released limitless possibilities of form and action. The whole population is being mobilised to tell the Story their way, throw out the politicians, stop the madness, change the world.

But wait a minute. There's a group who don't want change and they make the laws and control the capital. They don't believe in this collective rubbish. People are not intelligent enough to use theatre in this way. Give them picture newspapers to read, reality shows in which to participate, game-shows to play. Leave the question of what theatre should do and be about to those who know. This group clamps down on this radical form of theatre, channelling their vision into a narrow, sophisticated, literary form of words, attempting to suffocate the wild anarchic child at birth. But it's tough, this child. It will survive when they are long gone.

However, theatre in this new millennium has a problem. In many quarters it is perceived as, and indeed is, old-fashioned. That is both its strength and its weakness. While the 21st century internet communications highway powers along its technological, social media betwittered and facebooked path into a digitalised sunset, theatre remains two wanks and a soggy tissue. It cannot go forward, it cannot go back. It has nowhere to go, nowhere to run, nowhere to hide. All roads return to the same point. Theatre was, is, continues to be, a ceremonial circle, lassooing language – the last custodian and the embodiment of an oral tradition now threatened with extinction by soft-ware, hard-ware, any old where. Not that there aren't attempts to evolve, adapt, even rival its computerised confederates. Where once we whistled the set, now we sing the hydraulics.

And the problem is also social. Theatre often hides in dark corners of old buildings or cosies up in new. It has willingly crawled up an intellectual, middle-class fox-hole pursued by marketing hounds, refusing to come out even when attacked by ferocious terriers snarling in factories, railway arches, warehouses, disused pits. And even then the audience is often finite, educated, prescribed. Professional theatre teeters on the brink of its own grave, aided and abetted by an in-built philistinism. Can it be changed? Is it too late? Will it ever be a popular art form of the people? Was it ever? Does it need to be? I used to think theatre was the natural popular medium of expression, that through theatre the majority of the population would come to understand the nature of their lot. You know something? I still do.

4

To Begin at the Beginning

I was driving back from Milford Haven, having been present the night before at the opening of the newly refurbished Torch Theatre where the performance had been a mediocre production of Melvyn Bragg's musical *The Hired Man* transposed to Pembroke, when who should come on Radio 4 but the man himself. Melvyn banging on about *Henry VIII*. Yesterday his musical, today another exhibition of erudite wool-pulling. I'm sure he specialises in John Crace of *The Guardian*'s Potted Read.

Melvyn was a diligent member of the Board of the ESC for two years and I discovered later that we had coincided in the year I spent in Paris before going to Trinity College Dublin – though I suspect his experience was somewhat different from mine.

Cue.

For a spell in 1958 I was sports master, and also an occasional teacher of English, Mathematics (!) and History, at the École Anglaise de Paris, situated about thirty miles west of Paris at Andrésy. It was a school for the sons and daughters of SHAPE personnel (the Allied Forces) mostly American, but there was a total of seventeen nationalities of varying ages and abilities.

Not a lot of sport (of the athletic kind) was done – I did manage to achieve a couple of hand-springs and a football team that lost to a local school 25–19, me scoring 18 of our goals. My days were spent avoiding the Spanish teacher (male) and a series

23

of chunky American girls, bursting out of shorts and blouses. It was run by the Marquis de Kuègelain – a French resistance hero and my interview had been conducted by somebody called 'his son' who looked like a cross between Douglas Fairbanks Jnr. and Brad Pitt – impeccably mantled in a royal blue blazer, cravat and white shirt, collar turned up – a ringer for Christian in *Fifty Shades of Grey*. He turned to me, suave twenty-six facing callow nineteen and started working his mouth and nose as if desperately trying to withhold a sneeze.

Then, in a voice reminiscent of Oxford marmalade being strained through Terry Thomas, he said, mouth still working, nostrils flaring, 'Mm – you'll hev to – mm – ex-*cuse* may – mm – mm – Ay've – mm – got – a mouthful of toothpaste'.

It was a phrase I was to have occasion to use in the future when confronted by an inarticulate actor . . .

To raise money to get to Paris I sold my precious collection of British stamps, gathered over a period of ten years from the time I was nine. A couple of Penny Blacks, a load of Penny Reds and Twopenny Blues as well as a number of other valuable issues. This shark of a dealer gave me five pounds. It should have been about fifty but I was young, gullible and stupid. (So what has changed, the cry goes up? Everything. I'm no longer young.)

I also sold about one hundred of my father's books, including a load of his early Penguins. I don't know why my father let me do it – he prized books enormously, handled them with the utmost reverence. It's a mystery, and I prize books now just as highly, including his battered collection, yellow, nicotine stained from my mother's smoking. I can't even get rid of torn, thumbed old copies of *Penny Dreadfuls*. I wouldn't let my children do it. After I've gone OK.

I had booked a room in the Ecole Des Mines in the Rue St. Louis, a hostel for engineering students in the heart of the left bank, right by the Jardins de Luxembourg. The first evening I went down to the café below and was adopted by a group of engineers who were staying over in the hostel during the holiday period. They introduced me to a game called Cardinal Puff, which involved drinking copious amounts of red wine while trying to repeat a series of commands that Cardinal Puff uttered before taking a swig. The consequences were inevitable. I never looked back, spoke only French for six months and the only English friend I made was Maurice Frankel, now head of the Campaign for Freedom of Information, on a year's sabbatical from St. Andrews University.

I existed by playing my guitar around the cafes of the left bank – the Dome, the Selecte and the Coupole in Montparnasse, the corner by Odeon Metro on the Boulevard St. Germain, and Sartre's Café Flore. I was a three chord merchant, hopeless really, but I could wiggle my hips and thrust my pelvis in the appropriate manner and the streets resounded to the sound of *Blue Suede Shoes*, *Maybe Baby* and *Twenty Flight Rock* on a tinny old guitar. Elvis, Eddie Cochrane and Buddy Holly don't know what a debt I owe them. It was a novelty in those days, and the patrons generous, but with my severely limited repertoire I regularly attracted a modicum of opprobrium when I would come round the same three cafes an hour or so later with the same three songs.

But in this way I survived when the school packed up for the summer and I moved out of Les Mines. The diet was saucisses frites at La Petite Source on the Boulevard St. Germain and the treat was coeur brisé aux carottes in the Place du Pantheon, 90 centimes, serenaded by violin-playing Russian exile waiters. I must have slept on a floor in every street on the left bank, and a few nights in doorways as well.

I ate, drank, breathed and slept existentialism.

I hunted with Bernard and Marcel, two unemployed vagabonds, in the Jardins du Luxembourg. I discovered folk music in the underground cellar Le Batam in the Rue Cujas in the form of

Alex Campbell, a Scottish philanderer. I listened to jazz in Storyville and danced to Maxime Saury, both in the famed Rue De La Huchette, in the days before the street became pedestrianised for tourists seeking the authentic experience of a Turkish Kebab Shop, Algerian trinket rip-off merchants and real live students employed to dress up as existentialists.

Question. What does an existentialist look like?

I discovered the bookshop Shakespeare and Co. and ate soup in the back room in the company of Hemingway.

Le Fureur de Vivre. I was in love with life and love and thought I would never go back. Or go and live in Scandinavia. Ho, hum. TCD beckoned.

* * *

Cold October morning. That strange smell in the air – a combination of Liffy effluent at low tide, human and animal excrement. Lugging a brown suitcase along the cobble stones, threading between the cattle and the bicycles. A first night of madness passed, on that Irish phenomenon, the Liverpool package boat. Travelling steerage, a cabin awash with Guinness, snoring bogmen and wild singing, cows for companions. Fights.

I was in Dublin. A foreign land. In 1958. At that time Trinity was still a gentleman's university, a protestant oasis in the midst of a catholic cauldron. This beautiful college, catching at your heart and throat, at the heart of a city at the heart of a country. A cultural cocoon, a haven in the midst of poverty and literature, alcohol and animation. No girls allowed in college rooms after 6 pm, unless smuggled illegally in the boot of a car. Along with Butch from Birmingham I wore Teddy Boy drainpipes, a curiosity among the tweeds and cavalry twill of Oxbridge rejects.

A school colleague had written for application forms. A reply said just turn up on October 10th with £100.

A real place of learning. I wrote the same letter and received the same reply. Chance. It turned out to be the best thing I have ever done. I stayed eleven years.

Memories. An Irish girl. Long black hair and blue eyes. Sitting demurely at the table. Head scarf. Coat buttoned to the neck, handbag on the knees and drinking eight pints of Guinness without batting an eyelid. I drank five and fell over. I had met my first wife.

The Bailey. The phone ringing on the wall. Me answering.

'Is Mary Behan there?'

'Yes'.

'Tell her Brendan's gone.'

Bachelor parties in the Rubrics – college rooms; iron lungs of stout, and bicycles up the trees. After all night poker sessions walk to the Quays for an early morning pint.

Prompt at six, lights on, doors open, and there they are, the same familiar row of backs, hunched over black pints. 'You see lads, you can always get in round the side door. Unofficial like.'

The cold. The dirt. The beggars, tinkers. The smoke, the Guinness. The dance halls. Ten menless women to every legless man. The last waltz, a drunken rush of satisfaction. R.B.D. French, my tutor. And fortuitously the champion of Players, 'Try and get to a few more lectures . . .'

My brief-case, containing nothing but a pound of potatoes, a cauliflower and two whiting, bought in Moore Street for fourpence. Spilling and rolling down Grafton Street. Poker sessions with Mike Leahy, a politically incorrect philosophy student. His politically incorrect philosophy? Always go for the plainest girl in the room. A constant stream up and down his stairs – those same Ginger Man O'Keefe stairs at Number 3.

No. 3, the home of Players Theatre. My doom. Four years of misspent youth. Seating only fifty, and a stage bigger than the auditorium – writing, acting, directing. We took our revue, *Would Anyone Who Saw the Accident,* written by myself and Terry Brady, to The Theatre Royal, Stratford East. 'Yes I saw it', wrote Milton

Schulman, critic of *The Evening Standard*, 'the whole ghastly mess. And I'm a willing witness for the prosecution'.

My first brush with the London critics. I have lived to have many more.

There were twenty of us, a small but improbably talented bunch*. In it for the fun and world beaters.

We were prolific and profligate, whiling away our years and degrees in that dark corner of Front Square, ranting and raving ancient and modern, red-hot lovers of rotting curtains and musty doublets, staggering into the dawn of Botany Bay for an improbable bout of hang-over tennis. All spread far and wide now in the world of theatre, films and TV.

I lived in Oscar Wilde's rooms, briefly in Bram Stoker's. But then with only two hundred rooms and four hundred years of history you were bound to be preceded by someone famous. Goldsmith, Bourke, Sheridan, Synge, Berkley, Swift. I studied French under O'Sheehy Skeffington, son of a famous martyr, who studied under Beckett, who told a story of Rimbaud, discovering you could pull your eye out on a stalk – did so, waggling it around to get a strange distorted view of the world.

My waggling eye was Trinity and Dublin, the greatest un-training for life. I cried at the demise of Number 3. when they transferred it to an anonymous ill conceived space in the new Samuel Beckett Centre. An irreplaceable chunk of Trinity's – and my – life sacrificed on the altar of expediency. It should have a blue plaque slapped on it.

In that post-*Ginger-Man* period of '58 till '68 the world was full of TCD misfits wandering the globe not knowing what to do. So much yearning for Ireland that many returned or just simply stayed. I nearly did.

By chance (because he had asked me) I directed a one-act play in my penultimate year at TCD, written by Tony Aspler (later head of Canadian Radio –) entitled *Echo of a Sigh*. It won the Irish

Universities Drama Festival in Galway that year. I thought 'This is easy!' And directed *Huis Clos* by J.P. Sartre. It was terrible, notable only for me having passed over Bruce Myers and John Castle for the two male roles, both of whom left Trinity shortly after and went to RADA. Not as a result. But I was hooked.

I was lucky. I learnt the basics in the hard school of weekly rep, and explored area and space, lighting and staging, entrances and exits, apposition and counter-point through the medium of Revue. The latter was also the best school of dramaturgy of the lot – particularly if one were writing the show oneself. Opener, closer, first half climax, sketch versus musical number, whimsy versus blockbuster, the success of a traditional revue depended on a crucial balance of audience manipulation and extreme discipline. Do your own lighting, design your own sets. A training difficult to get these days. Invaluable. And in a way, safer than fucking up plays and actors.

It soon became clear, however, that if I were to make my way in Dublin my quizzical, existential view of the world would be better expressed through directing plays, rather than by writing sketches about Eamonn Andrews and doing take-offs of the Everly Brothers (rather good ones, though I say it myself) or writing revues with titles such as *Cucu jug jug, puwee, Nuts in May* and *Baked Beans and Cold Rice Pudding* etc.

I formed a company with the late Ralph Bates, a fine actor whose triumphs were mostly confined to screen and television, and Joanna van Gysegham, the grand-daughter of Johnston Forbes Robertson and the daughter of Jean Forbes Robertson and Andre van Gysegham, a founder of the Unity Theatre. Ralph and Jo were sleeping partners (literally – they married, with me as best man), responsible for putting up the money. The Company was resident at the Gas Company Theatre, Dun Laoghaire – Kingstown as it was known to the residents of this leafy port some ten miles south of Dublin where the boat comes in from

Holyhead. On many a grey dawn have I seen, with relief, the church spires thrusting towards the Wicklow mountains after a night spent throwing up.

The Gas Company Theatre was situated in Dun Laoghaire High Street (it is now a cafe). The entrance was through the gas cookers in the showroom to a lecture auditorium at the back, seating some two hundred. Above the stage, embroidered in gold on a red velvet pelmet, in letters 6 ft high, was the word 'GAS'. The stage was seventeen feet wide by twelve deep with no way round the back. It was here that throughout the fifties the Globe Theatre Company operated, with talent such as Godfrey Quigley, Norman Rodway, Donal Donnelly, Paddy Bedford, Maureen Toal, Anna Manahan, Pauline Delaney, Jack McGowran and others. The Company moved to the Gate Theatre, Dublin, in the sixties, and then most of them to London.

We set up shop here in '64, doing it all ourselves. On Saturday afternoons, it would be down to the pier and give away tickets or sell 3 for 1, 4 for 1 – anything . . . Audiences were on the youthfully challenged side. The buzzing of hearing aids interfered with the lights (all six of them), the two end seats of each row were removed to make way for the wheel chairs and a wheeze could be easily confused with a laugh.

One day Teddy Rhodes rode into town, an actor in wolf's clothing. He convinced me that the play, *Wolf's Clothing,* would pack them in (to coffins, I remarked – cynically). It was my first encounter with the professional's professional. He gave me the run around. He'd done the play (and the part) about a hundred times and knew all the tricks and a few more. I became more and more humiliated. Wasn't I supposed to be the director? Wasn't he supposed to listen to me? Why were all my ideas so wrong? With ego bumps sprouting like Brussels all over my psyche, I finally shouted (blush, blush, shame, shame) 'If you're so bloody clever, then you can do it all without me!' and I stormed out and sat in the pub waiting for them to come and fetch me, prostrate themselves, pathetically beg my forgiveness, pleading that they couldn't continue without me.

I sat there for an hour. Just one pint. Then I went to the cafe for half an hour. A cup of tea. Then, abjectly, I crept back into the theatre at the back of the auditorium. They were already on to the second act. I moved down a few rows. Then a few more. Finally, from about Row 4, I made a remark. Everyone carried on as if nothing had happened. Nobody even mentioned the incident. I vowed that never again would I indulge myself in fits of pique; that, if feeling vulnerable, I would take a deep breath, stay calm and work my way through it. This is a rule I've applied to this day. It is easy to be hurt. Under pressure, many people say cruel things. Either grin and bear it or give back as good as you can get. Sometimes difficult if the actor, Bill Wallis, is fifty yards away down The Cut, retreating from the Young Vic Theatre, shouting 'You're a bastard, Bogdanov'.

'So are you' doesn't quite have the same pith about it.

In 1965 I got the job of assistant electrician (!) on the touring production of *Stephen D* by Hugh Leonard, the play that first brought Norman Rodway and T P McKenna to London. It was directed by Jim Fitzgerald, who, in the space of six weeks, taught me more about lighting than I had learnt before or since. He took me through the lamps, the gels, the focusing, the effects, all in the process of three days technically mounting the show. A wonderful director, a wonderful teacher, a wonderful man with a drink problem. He went on a bender in Zurich. I was the only member of the company who could speak German. The set had been impounded due to a strike in Liverpool. The technical team in the Zuricher Schauspielhaus went to work and in thirty-six hours had produced a better set than the one we had left behind, which had taken three weeks to build . . . in Paris, Fitz went missing altogether. I was the only one who could speak French. I had to take over as director, staging the show, doing the lighting, giving notes. From humble beginnings . . . and all on £2 10s a week. The lowest wage in the Company.

When I got back to Dublin, Brendan Smith, avuncular Chef of the Dublin Theatre Festival, showed his appreciation. He gave me a fiver. It pays to speak other languages.

Ten years in Ireland taught me a life-long love of Irish traditional music, from the moment in 1959 at the Wexford Festival, when the door of the snug of the Waterfront Bar burst open and three strapping lads carrying a Tricolour, burst in and, standing to attention, sang *Kevin Barry*. It was the anniversary of the Wexford Martyr's hanging. I shrank in the corner, a blue Brit in a blue shit. They then sat down and ran through the gamut of songs that were to become standards, *Whiskey in the Jar*, *The Quare Bungle Rye*, *The Holy Ground* – accompanied by a Bodhran player (skin drum), a fiddler and a tin whistle player who materialised at different times from nowhere. I was hooked.

For a spell I had my own radio programme on RTE, singing original compositions laced with traditional ballads. It was called 'Rhythm and Roundelay' and featured André Prieur and the Casino Orchestra, all six of them. He'd do a number, I'd do a number. In between I would come up with pithy comments on the week's events – a sort of poor man's Ned Sherrin. I was performing throughout an Equity strike. I didn't realise that I was being a black leg. One week the programme went out nine times. Every time I turned the radio on, there was this voicing trilling – 'I am a weary and a lonesome traveller' – to the sound of three chords on a tinny guitar bought for £4 off a man who was emigrating to Alaska to look for gold. (True.)

The summer of '62 I got smashed up in a car crash, hitching back from Paris, was hospitalized in Abbeville, finished my finals four months late, ending up in plaster up to my thigh. I had been due to return to Britain in the autumn to write a TV series for

ATV with Terry Brady and here I was, still in Dublin in deepest January, on crutches, with the snow knee deep. John Molloy, an angular mime artist came to my rescue, asking me to write a few sketches for a Revue he was doing at The Gate Theatre – *Say Nothin'*. And that is how I met The Dubliners.

The Dubliners – 'The force that through the green fuse drives the flower . . .' – at once proof of a life to be lived and the absurdity of it. Ronnie Drew, a voice like crushed coke (the black kind) and Barney McKenna were the first two members of the group. Barney would sit on a stool in O'Donoughue's, twenty pints to the bad, and play his banjo like a god. He was a telephone wire repairer. One day a pole fell on his foot and he was off for six weeks. Every time he had to report to the Doctor, he would hit his toe with a hammer . . . he hadn't worked for nine months. But he had played his banjo.

I was the first to put The Dubliners on stage in a show entitled 'The Hootenanny Ballad and Blues Show', also at the Gate Theatre. Also performing were Dominic Behan, brother of Brendan, and Alex Campbell, the Scottish folk singer who I had first met in Paris in the Spring of 1958. My Existential period

The show was my first encounter with Luke Kelly. He had just returned to Ireland from a stint of working on the sites in Britain. 'For we need the money your Daddy earns on England's motorways' he sang. Luke was bull-sturdy, his head too big for his shoulders, a flame-red shock of hair and beard. He stood on the stage as if rooted to a rock, hands in pockets and sang . . . you could feel the collective shiver thrill up the collective spine. He's dead now – the drink. I chose Luke's 'The Rocky Road to Dublin' for Desert Island Discs in his memory. He once said to Patsy, my wife – 'You're full of babies'. He was right.

For a spell I was the Dubliners' roadie. Basically, that meant going on ahead, looking at the venue, sorting out the two or three rusty lamps – old Rob Roy arc-lights – clearing the stage and then re-tracing the road to find out which pub they were in. I had it down to a fine art. Look at the map, estimate the amount of time, diminishing, between stops for a drink, and then search every hostelry within a ten mile stretch. They defeated me only once.

We were in a barn of an old cinema in Limerick, seating two thousand. Curtain up (I use the term loosely) at 8 o'clock. Map out, calculate the route, off I set. Nowhere. I returned at 9.00 p.m. The crowd was somewhat restless. At 9.30, I made an announcement. They broke the place up. I caught up with the boys the next day back in town. They had got as far as the Red Cow in Naas, some twenty miles outside Dublin and hadn't moved.

We arrived at one point in Mullingar for the Fladh Ceogh, the National climax of a series of local music and dance festivals that take place all over Ireland, – the exuberant, drunken, equivalent of the Welsh Eisteddfod. It was Friday afternoon. We got stuck into a small snug in a bar and started playing. And drinking bottles of stout. Saturday morning I left to go back to Dublin to do some editing of a TV programme at Radio Telefis Eireann. I returned on Saturday evening. They were still where I had left them. The bottles were river deep, mountain high. Barney was slumped against the wall, still playing. Ceiran Bourke, now also dead, still whistling. John Sheehan, tee-total, drinking orange juice, still fiddling. Ronnie, still croaking.

They went through that Saturday night and Sunday morning. I laid them out to sleep in a field on Sunday afternoon, then drove them back to Dublin. Ronnie died in 2008 of throat cancer. He used to sleep under my bed – I still have a pair of his winklepickers somewhere *circa* 1965. Another chunk of my life erased. The older, the narrower the memories become. The circle of wagons gets ever smaller and the Indians are closing in.

I was an amateur drinker in Ireland. Irish whisky and Guiness. 'An Irishman is the only man in the world who'll climb over twelve naked women to get to a bottle of stout' (Anon). The creative energy and sheer joy of singing and storytelling is infectious and the bug, once caught, never leaves you. Irish unpredictability, the unorthodox, skew-whiff approach to logic and life, leaves you breathless at the sheer audacity of minds that leap, twist, flash and turn like salmon at the falls. The frustrating side of this was captured in Hilton Edwards' (founder with Michael MacCliamoir of the Gate Theatre) exasperated remark that 'the Irish and the Dutch should change places. In no time, the Dutch would turn this scraggy, chaotic, fertile land into an agricultural paradise and, at the same time, the Irish would forget to fill in the holes in the dykes and drown'. Brendan Behan said to me once 'If it was raining soup, the Irish would come out with forks'.

After ten years in Ireland I have a horror of doing Irish plays with any actors other than Irish. The English try to pin down the elusive Celtic butterfly soul with a sledgehammer. The Irish leap-frog England to middle Europe, the last vestiges of a culture and a language that was once spoken the length and breadth of the continent. The deep, dark despair, the laughter and tears, storytelling and music, the religion, the politics, a sense of the cultural belonging that is once again manifesting itself in Latvia, Lithuania, Rumania. . . . It is a world strongly alien to the English psyche, unfathomable, deeply mysterious and one which, to be honest, they are not very interested in . . . until they go there. I love them.

I woke up when I was twenty-nine. I had been eleven years in Dublin and was beginning to quarrel with Ireland politically, religiously and socially. It was the beginning of the Troubles – passionate speeches in Irish from table tops in the canteen. It was time to leave. I had enjoyed my stint as a Producer/Director in RTE but I hankered after theatre. When I was offered yet another live Showband Show on the road (they wouldn't let me do drama – I was the clown who wanted to play Hamlet) I loaded wife, son and Hoover into the car and headed back to Wales. Ireland – Wales? One Celtic cocoon for another.

* * *

My family is from Neath – Castell Nedd in Welsh, Neath Castle – a stone's throw from Abertawe, 'The Mouth of the River Tawe', Dylan Thomas' ugly, lovely town of Swansea. We left when I was three, my mother taking us up to join my father in the East End of London at the height of the Blitz. The bombs were preferable to living with her mother. I returned to my native land in 1969 at the age of thirty searching for a place to live with wife, family and dog and eventually found it.

I crested the brow of a small pitch and there it was, nestling in the sunlight below me, the front half hidden by a profusion of runner beans and chrysanthemums. Tafarn-y-Crydd – The Shoe-makers Arms Pentrebach, a pub four miles north of Sennybridge, Breconshire, on the lonely edge of the Mynydd Epynt. This was once the largest and highest area of mountain plateau sheep farming in the British Isles. Now it is an Army range – its fields pock-marked and scarred by shells, the walls of its scattered farm-houses blackened with the fires of raw recruits huddling for warmth among the ruins. Where once Welsh was borne on the winds and the backs of Epynt ponies the voices of York, Lancaster, Birmingham and Belfast compete with the cries of hawk and kite. Though sheep may still safely graze (relatively), bullets lay claim to the freedom of the air.

It was September 1969. Six weeks later we moved in – my wife and I and two small children of eighteen months and six weeks. People came from miles around to see the new owners, Saturday lunchtime, handing the furniture over heads, through the bar and up through a hatch in the floor to the interconnected bedrooms above. A total of thirty six children had been born up there in the conjunctive brass and wooden bed, retained at our request.

This was the first time the pub had passed out of the hands of the Williams family in one hundred years. A two storey Welsh cottage, the front room a bar. Hand-tapped beer and poured from a jug. No toilet, empty the Elsan in the stream that ran past the door.(Oh dear!) Sunday was a tin bath in front of the fire.

I fell in love with the people, the culture, the valley. Champion shearers, hedgers, sewers, bakers – the remnants of that Epynt way lived on in the Cilieni and Eithrin valleys, their meeting point the Shoemakers Arms. Births, marriages, deaths, anniversaries, the sports, the choir, the parish council, the trip to Cardiff, Phantom, Smithfield – all emanated, took place, were celebrated, planned and executed from that small bar. Nothing north, east or west for twelve miles. Except sheep, snow, rain, wind. . . . Sennybridge, that bursting metropolis of five hundred souls, a lifetime away four miles down below. We are talking serious community here.

The backs grew straighter, the pints held tighter, the voices swell. What started at 10pm as an isolated sporadic assault on the aural senses, within half an hour has soared to a joyous crescendo of deep, high mellifluous harmonies. The babble and banter of sheep and potatoes, beetroot and hedging, tractors and trout, is stilled as the bar pays homage to the unmistakable music of the Welsh male voice.

'Hwyl' – an untranslatable Welsh word for a mood of togetherness, longing, a community communing. Will Garth, Dai Cefn, John Garth, Alwyn Nantsebon, Vivian the Rhiw – all known by the names of the farms they live in – their ruddy capped faces pressed clear-eyed together, and the more drink taken the better the sound. Hymns, songs of love, praise of the Lord; the Chapel upbringing running deep in the psyche of the Welsh spirit. A curious mixture, the Lord and alcohol, and deep in the Celtic soul amid the laughter and delight, a mystic yearning that brings tears. Mae hen wlad fy nhadau – Land of my Fathers.

A million people speak Welsh as a first language. It has withstood the ravages and assaults of Romans, Angles, Saxons, Brits and latterly everything that Television could throw at it, to survive, dark and beautiful in the hills and valleys from Carreg Cennan to Cader Idris and on a Saturday night, on high days and feast days, in hostelries north and south such as Tafarn y Crydd – The Shoemakers Arms, Pentrebach, Llandeilo'r Fan, a community of some fifty souls nestling on the slopes of the Mynydd Eppynt (Mountain of Wild Ponies). Welsh song born on the wings of ale and stout, bands a land together that forever keeps a laughing welcome in its hillsides.

For I know that when I walk back in that pub within minutes I shall be laughing like I never laugh anywhere else in the world. The capacity of the people – born together, living together, dying together – to enjoy each others company, day in day out, never ceases to fill me with wonder and amazement. Even when up to their eyeballs in sheep-shit, their necks in mud, their chins in water and their shoulders in snow they'll still be laughing. In Llandeilo'rfan. Population fifty-six.

After six months of running The Shoemakers Arms I rang Terry Hands, who was then an Associate and Director of Theatre-Go-Round at the RSC, a position I had been offered a year earlier, but the money had run out. Terry and I were old friends from his Liverpool Everyman days where I had directed my very first production on English soil, my own musical version of Moliere's *The Hypochondriac*, set in the twenties.

'Any jobs going?', I asked.

'We're interviewing for assistant directors tomorrow, get up here as fast as you can'.

They were all there, a full house of the RSC Directorate, – John Barton, Trevor Nunn, Terry, David Jones. I laid down the law about the educational role of theatre. They didn't seem very impressed. I went back to be a publican in the Welsh hills thinking I'd blown it. The next day, Terry rang to say I'd got the job, start immediately. For two years I commuted.

* Terry Brady actor extraordinaire and my co-writer; Ralph Bates, tragically died early, star of *Poldark*, and Hammer hero; Roger Cheveley, later Head of Design Yorkshire TV; John Gardener, Administrator of the Liverpool Everyman and the Leicester Haymarket; Roger Ordish, The Jimmy Saville Spherical Order of Merit for Service Beyond the Call of Duty for twenty-five years Producer of *Jim'll Fix it* (I am not sure how he feels now . . .); Bruce Myers, for forty years – and still – Peter Brook's leading actor; John Castle, left to star in *The Lion in Winter* opposite Peter O'Toole; Shane Bryant, another Hammer hero; Martin Lewis, BBC announcer and *News at Ten;* and . . . and . . . and . . . and I haven't even got to Jo van Gysegham, Max Stafford Clark, Gillian Hannah, Dinah Stabb . . .)

5

Assistant to Peter Brook

Peter Brook once said to me – 'Charles Marowitz was the best assistant I ever had'. His small white hands, hardly those of a 'hard handed man' fluttered in a characteristic gesture and he laughed: 'Whatever he said I always did the opposite. It invariably worked'.

Being an assistant director is usually a thankless task – make the tea, run errands, audition the children. I've done all these things and sometimes find myself asking others to do them. And yet used creatively, an assistant director may make a massive contribution to the success of a piece of work. If you make the assumption that the constant companion at your shoulder is not a rival for your job or planning to take over the production by inciting the company to mutiny, then he or she can provide you with valuable support, acting as a catalyst, a sounding-board for ideas and discussion. The roll-call of assistants I've had makes for impressive reading: Jude Kelly, Sean Holmes, Charley Hanson, Antonia Bird, Tim Carroll, Justin Greene, Jonathan Church, Tim Baker, Michael Attenborough, Sue Pomeroy, Giles Block. . . .

So, in 1970 I became an Assistant Director at the RSC. The real world . . . I was one and a half years there, at thirty the oldest assistant they had ever had. At £25 a week and with two small children it was 100% drop in salary from my wage in TV; was I sure that I wanted to do it, they asked. I knew that if I were going to begin again in theatre, I would have to get to grips with

40

Shakespeare. It made sense to go to the one place where they knew more about Shakespeare than anywhere else in the world. So I thought.

Terry, responsible for getting me there in the first place, handed the children over to me to work with in his production of *Richard III* with Norman Rodway in the title role, and treated any ideas I had with icy contempt.

Trevor Nunn whispered to Alan Howard (*Hamlet*) in corners, the play set in the ice and snow of mid-winter in what became known as the 'polar bear Hamlet' due to the heavy white fur coats that clad the entire cast, and to this day I don't know what Trevor thought the play was about.

John Barton mumbled and stumbled his way through directing *Measure for Measure*, revealed himself surprisingly not to be the pedant that the theatre world had come to see him as, but extremely theatrical and willing to admit when stumped. He gave me the prison scene to direct. I tried to involve the whole company in the 'dance of the lunatics' – the entrance of the inmates with Ben Kingsley, Claudio, leading a chorus of 'The fit's upon me now'. Ian Richardson, Angelo, wisely ducked out of this exercise in democratic ensemble commitment. John Barton looked horrified when I unveiled this piece of non-naturalistic nonsense to him. He puffed on his cigarette, removed it, scratched his beard and then stuck his cigarette back in his mouth the wrong way round. Maybe it was the burnt tongue that stopped him properly questioning the intention behind the scene. It found its way into performance. John never did have the heart to tell me that it just didn't fit with his production.

Robin Phillips, director of *The Two Gentlemen of Verona* couldn't cope with Philip Manikum as Speed – they seemed to talk at cross purposes all the time – and handed his scenes over to me. I was on Phil's wavelength, able to follow his quirky way of communicating at one brain removed. I got to rehearse all the

Launce and Speed scenes with Patrick Stewart. And a real dog. I turned Phil into a beach vendor, baseball cap, Bermuda shorts, dark glasses, a vending tray, whistle in his mouth, and a football rattle which he whirled incessantly as he cried 'Cacouettes! Cacouettes!' The rattle kept disappearing. Each time I asked the stage management team for it, the reply was that they didn't know where it had gone. I bought two new ones during the course of rehearsals, before realising that they were hiding them from me. Robin hated it. I now know why.

John Barton and Robin Phillips co-directed a production of *The Tempest*, or rather, John did, while Robin looked sulkily on. It was here, during one of those extended technical note sessions for which Stratford was famous during previews, where we were counter-productively up all night for the third time running, that I achieved the ultimate in assistant directorial insensitivity. I suggested at 3.30 a.m. to Christopher Morley (designer) that the log that Ferdinand was carrying looked like Snoopy (it did). Chris went berserk, throwing chairs, shouting and running screaming all around the old Conference Hall rehearsal room (now the Swan Theatre). John puffed on his cigarette, Robin played with his beads and Trevor Nunn gazed unblinkingly at the floor. Chris sat down and we carried on as normal.

Which leaves Peter Brook and *A Midsummer Night's Dream*.

It was enormously fortuitous that my time as assistant coincided with that of one of the great theatre magicians of the twentieth century returning to the RSC to work on one of the great seminal productions of that era. For close on three years I lived and breathed that production, long after I had left Stratford. I worked on the London transfer, spent three weeks working on my own with the replacements for the New York run, passed the summer in Paris as Associate re-rehearsing at the Gobelins for the World Tour, and had the good fortune to visit the production world wide to supervise both the 'get-in' and to take notes, flying at one point from St. Paolo in Brazil, where I was directing *Os Dos Caballeros di Verona* (*The Two Gentlemen of Verona*) to Chicago and back again over a week-end.

(The first day at the Gobelins had begun with a disaster. Terry Taplin, Lysander, eager to try out the physical possibilities of the set, stupidly vaulted from the top of the walkway down to the floor below. It was solid concrete. Terry crushed both his heels. I had to ferry him in my battered Morris Minor Convertible, top down, Terry upended on the back seat, legs dangling out the back, across Paris to the American Hospital where he was operated on, a dozen thin plates being inserted in his heels to build them up again. He was unable to walk for six months. Bruce Myers replaced him at short notice.)

Shakespeare's play is nominally set in Athens and a fairy-inhabited forest nearby. Brook took as his starting point Jan Kott's essay on *A Midsummer Night's Dream* in his book *Shakespeare Our Contemporary*, where Kott explores the overt sexuality of the play as emphasised by Oberon's degrading of Titania in coupling her with an ass. Kott emphasises the fact that a donkey is possessed with significant procreative equipment – the biggest cock in the corral. 'Come, tie up my lover's tongue' cries Tiatania – no more talking – 'lead him to my bower. Let's fuck'. At this point David Waller was hoisted onto Hugh Keyes-Byrne's shoulder, who thrust his arm with a bunched fist through David's legs in the simulation of a massive erect phallus while the music of Mendelssohn's *Wedding March* blared out in a completely other context.

The second element that informed his thinking was the 'dream' as a self-induced drug trip, with its emphasis on a magic mushroom type trip contained in the mind-blowing properties of the 'little purple flower'. This complete rejection of any sense of the 19th and 20th century tradition, led to a focus on the play being located in 'the heightened realm of metaphor'. The aim was to do away with what Brook called bad tradition and open up the play to a new experience so that both the actors and the audience could feel that they were encountering the text for the first time.

The set, designed by Sally Jacobs with whom Peter had collaborated on many a venture, was a three sided white box with no ceiling, two doors in the back wall, and a walkway running all the way round with wall ladders at strategic points for on-stage access. It resembled nothing more than a squash court and was described variously as 'a drive-on bicycle ferry', 'a trainee driver's tank and 'Alcatraz'. The Production was likened to 'Eskimo Nell on Ice' and 'The Boilerman's Entertainment in Hold Eleven'. In Stratford, black borders were hung to hide the lighting; after Stratford we decided to remove them, leaving the lighting bars and stage machinery visible. The purpose of the set, with its upper balcony and two entrances upstage, was to echo the simplicity of the Elizabethan thrust stage (although we were playing in the conventional proscenium of the Stratford Memorial Theatre) an experiment followed through at the RSC in the construction of The Swan, The Courtyard, and the redesign of the current Royal Shakespeare Theatre. Instead of the Wooden O, the Wooden Oblong, with the text being paramount and the physical aids few. This approach was mixed with modern elements, the trees of the forest being represented by coils of retractable wire which could be let down from above by the 'fairies' or, as they were known, the AVs – the audio-visuals. Titania's bower was a huge red feather, suspended in view by four wires.

The inspiration for the fairy magic, and indeed the basis for the whole production, was a group of Chinese acrobats, which Peter and Sally had seen in Paris the year before and who presented themselves to the audience in dazzling white silk costumes. Oberon entered on a trapeze, and the love potion that Puck fetches, the 'little purple flower', was a similarly coloured spinning plate on a rod, which Puck passed to Theseus also from a trapeze fifteen feet above the stage. Puck tormented the lovers striding the stage on six feet stilts and when Bottom was transformed into an ass, he acquired not an asses head, but a black ping-pong ball nose and a pair of round micky-mouse ears.

The AVs wielded long, ridged, flexible tubes called 'Freekas' which when whirled emitted a strange low or high pitched moaning/whistling sound depending on how forcefully they were twirled. I was charged with tracking them down to their manufacturing source which turned out to be a firm in Florida. With Peter standing by I told the firm they were to be sent to the Royal Shakespeare Company. 'What State is that in?' they asked. I repeated the remark to Peter. 'Heh, heh, heh!' he laughed, 'a terrible state!'.

Peter had wanted to perform the last scene of *The Dream* entirely by candle light, in an approximation of how it would have been lit in a Jacobean indoor production at the Blackfriars Theatre. Five hundred candles were standing by. However the fire regulations put the kybosh on the idea and we were reduced to a token symbol of one candle only, the stage being lit in bright white artificial light. Brook was praised for it. Art by accident . . .

The costumes were neither Athenian, nor Renaissance nor essentially modern, and reflected Brook's preoccupation with psychedelia and the acid/pot drug culture of the time. Theseus/Oberon wore a purple satin gown, Hippolyta/Titania a primary green one and Puck a bright yellow satin jumpsuit. The lovers looked like 1960s 'flower children' in tie-dye shirts and ankle-length dresses. The Mechanicals were dressed as 20th-century artisans.

With the AVs Brook broke with the tradition of the fairies being played by young children or all women. He cast two women and two men, dressed in anonymous beige-grey tops and trousers, an effect described as 'disconcertingly strange and threatening'. The forest became a more frightening, adult place than in earlier productions, particularly in the scene of Hermia's nightmare where she became entangled in the coils of wire wielded by the AVs from above.

The doubling of the roles of Theseus/Oberon, Hippolyta/Titania and Philostrate/Puck was only partly to create a smaller, more intimate company: mainly it was to suggest that they were not so much different characters, as different aspects of the human characters' personalities. With Theseus/ Oberon and Hippolyta/Titania this is entirely sustainable. Peter believed that Theseus and Hippolyta had failed to achieve 'the true union as a couple' and therefore worked through their quarrels subconsciously as Oberon and Titania.

With Philostrate/Puck doubling his theory was based on the fact that both are in effect MCs – the organisers of the revels (in Puck's case inadvertently) – and that Philostrate remarks that he has been a witness to the Mechanicals' rehearsal, something we know that Puck has seen but no-one else. The quartet of double roles was completed by Aegeus/Quince. The case for this is somewhat more nebulous, hinging on the fact that both characters are catalysts for the action: Aegeus for the main play in setting off the events that follow his demand that Hermia marry Lysander against her wishes, and Quince, as director and initiator of the play within the play.

One further innovation. At the conclusion, as Oberon spoke his final lines, 'Meet me all by break of day', the house lights slowly rose, so that members of the audience were visible to each other. Puck then spoke the play's closing speech and, reinterpreting the line 'Give me your hands, if we be friends' not to mean applause, the entire cast, led by him, came down into the auditorium to shake hands with the audience, uniting performer and spectator in an act of communal celebration.

Peter was the first director at the RSC to treat me as an equal, ask my opinion, listen, take me with him to all planning meetings where he took a perverse delight in deflecting questions my way that were put to him. 'What do you think Michael?' Peter was a confirmation of many things that up to that moment I had instinctively grasped, but had little or no occasion to put into practice. He is unafraid of experiment, of going up blind alleys, improvising, using all kinds of exercises to stretch and expand mind and body. He built up a sense of the text through a ruthless investigation of the sub-text, elevating it onto another level, spiritual, subliminal, by the systematic elimination of false emotions and values, challenging the actors to go further and deeper into themselves than ever before, exposing parts of their psyche that had remained buried within. If you followed him on this journey into the unknown, the result could be either exhilarating or terrifying; if you didn't, you took refuge in the tricks of the trade. Notable dissenters were Chris Gable, Norman Rodway and Terence Hardiman, all three of whom withdrew from the production after the Stratford run and were replaced for New York and London.

It was dangerous, this release of primal energy, a fact that I was acutely aware of in the years to come in employing similar methods. Actors out of control of their minds and their bodies are a danger to others and to themselves. Tampering with the psychological makeup, asking them to put themselves totally in your hands is a precious trust that cannot be abused. When it is – that way madness lies, and before *The Dream* was over there had been a suicide and several breakdowns.

For Brook was also a destroyer. Mary Rutherford (Hermia) suffered particularly from the lash of his tongue. 'This is a descent into suburbia' Brook said to her, eyes unblinking, a cold blue. 'A TV play of mumbled intimacy, a Stratford bus stop meeting. Where is the emotional life of it? Where is the vibration of words? Where is your line through it? You can't play a sub-text in Shakespeare at the wrong moment as you can in any fucking, ordinary naturalistic drama. At this stage of rehearsal you're wasting your time and ours as well.' And more in that vein. Mary was destroyed, but survived to produce one of the great physical images of the production as she flew sideways, parallel to the ground, to get jammed across the doorway by a fleeing Lysander. She was later to play Juliet for me in my own seminal (for me) production of *Romeo and Juliet* at the Leicester Haymarket Theatre. (See my Introduction to the new edition of *Shakespeare The Director's Cut.*)

In retrospect, I learned several things from this experience. For example, in British theatre very few people speak to each other with honesty and openness, saying exactly what they think of behaviour, performance, attitude. This sense of reticence and the belief of some directors that they must be all things to all persons makes one forget how civilised the rehearsal process is in Britain. Perhaps the shortness of the rehearsal period has something to do with it – we just don't have time to get stuck into ball-breaking rows that go on for weeks. 'The English have an extraordinary ability for flying into a great calm'.

When I first went to Germany in 1986 to direct *Julius Caesar* at the Deutsches Schauspielhaus, Hamburg, I was horrified to hear actors say aggressively to each other in voices that the English would call shouting – 'What you're doing there is crap!' 'Well what the fuck did you think you were doing in that last scene, I've never seen such a wank in my life'. (All in German of course). I would interpose myself anxiously, expecting blows at any minute. More would join in, until everything calmed down of its own accord and rehearsals continued as normal, everyone the best of friends. Nobody took the slightest offence. It took me a while to get used to this level of honest interchange, but after a time I embraced it enthusiastically. I had a wonderful feeling of release, of being able to say directly what I thought without giving offence and without beating around the bush for some euphemistic way of being critical for fear of hurting someone's sensibility. German actors are, in fact, very supportive of each other, a feeling born of the ensemble system, of working with the same people for many years, from theatre to theatre, sometimes for a lifetime.

This hard-hitting way of expressing themselves – directors ditto – is born of mutual knowledge, trust, and faith in each others ability. This is a far cry from Brook's attempt to open out a disparate group of English actors brought together for one season, of differing backgrounds, experience and training, totally unused to such a confrontational technique. And yet obviously this degree of honesty is something to which each group should aspire, born of that trust. There is no call to attack and wound someone personally in order to be truthful, but there is a need for a ruthless analysis of intention allied to result and, where the result is found wanting, a minute examination of all the contributory factors must follow. If this involves taking to pieces an actor's technique or a director's motives then that is what is required. Both actor and director must build up an inner strength to combat any personal sense of assault that may be lurking beneath the surface. After all, we should all have a common aim in mind – to produce a stunning piece of theatre where the sum total of the parts is greater than any one contribution. Theatre as a communal process. And *A Midsummer Night's Dream* was all of that.

The second thing I discovered was that, despite the success of *The Dream* – the wondrous, joyous, exuberant celebration of theatricality of the whole thing – there was a political side to the play in which Brook did not appear to be terribly interested.

What was it that he missed? In the nightmarish drug-fuelled psychedelian Chinese Circus Zeitgeist of a production that Brook conjured up at no point was there a real investigation of the repressive, tyranical regime of Theseus, a society that abuses women – marry the choice of your father or it's the chop – or at best a pair of knee pads for the rest of your life. This is a constant theme throughout the cannon, and one that marks Shakespeare out as an egalitarian and a feminist. I became more and more conscious of this lack as I watched performance after performance get funnier and funnier with any sense of danger and darkness receding with each gale of laughter. Maybe it's that our awareness and sensitivity to gender politics has changed enormously in the intervening period, but nevertheless it is strange in a play that is such a powerful analysis of the battle between the male and the female psyche that the gender politics were of little interest to him.

Finally, I learnt that it is never too late to change

On the day of the fourth preview, Brook stripped down the first act from top to bottom, completely re-staging the scenes. The Mechanicals' rehearsal scene in particular, which Peter believed should be improvisational, was never resolved in his mind, and he attempted till the end to find an orchestrated solution for a strictly controlled scene that would *look* as if it were improvised. The Mechanicals' Burgomask dance at the end of the play Peter entrusted to the actors themselves. The group would come back with their latest attempt and Peter would shake his head and try to intellectually articulate what he was seeing in his head which seemed to be a celebration of a combination of clog-dance, lederhosen and jig. Completely baffled the actors would go away and try again. And again. And again. Until at last Peter cried 'That's it!', proving that direction is not necessarily a case of knowing what you want but of knowing what you *don't* want.

The down side of this approach is the confusion it causes among the actors. A constant complaint, echoed in the corridors and canteen was – 'He makes us do things so many different ways we never know what he wants. He takes us apart in little pieces and then leaves us to put ourselves together again'.

Frankie de la Tour (Helena): When I think I'm being good, he says I'm bad. When I think I'm being terrible he says I'm marvellous. I don't know what to think any more.

A typical exchange:

Ralph Cotterill (AV): Tell us what this play is about.

Brook: I'll tell you after the first performance. It's a fairy tale. It can mean anything you like.

Mary Rutherford (Hermia): You don't seem to like it when I'm acting – only when I do nothing.

Brook: If doing nothing is acting then do nothing because when you act you do nothing for me.

B-boom!

On the day of the penultimate preview, Peter went through the second act doing the same thing as he had done with the first – changing, cutting, re-staging the comic business. This after three months rehearsal, then an exceptional length of time in the English system (it is still). It is axiomatic in theatre, I suppose, that however long one rehearses – a week, a month, a year – however organically the relationships and moves develop during rehearsal, in the final analysis staging always comes down in the end to 'can you cheat it a little bit further down stage left?' Or 'One pace forward and you'll find the light' (all together now, children – 'If you can see the light, the light can see you!')

Even the wearing of the same costumes for the famous psychological doubling of Theseus/Oberon and Hippolyta/Titania was a last minute accident – Peter was dissatisfied with the costumes and the wire, silver and copper wigs of Oberon and Titania and these were abandoned at the preview stage in favour of the Kings and Queens of mortals and myth wearing just the one outfit: Alan acquiring a purple satin gown in place of his white, and both using their own hair instead of the wire wigs which were supposed to differentiate them from the mortals. 'They're the same people really, aren't they?', Peter said to me, 'One's just the dark side of the other . . .'. Art by accident and a legend (and a casting imperative) were born.

Puck too was transformed by a change out of his dowdy beige into a bright, lemon-yellow jump suit.

So. Never be afraid of change. Just two days before the London opening Brook arrived at the Aldwych Theatre to supervise the final rehearsals.

Now the Aldwych sightlines are notorious. From the back of the stalls the highest visible point on stage stands at nine feet. (I'm talking in old money as the story is in the past.) The balcony scene in Romeo and Juliet in a now notorious production was invisible for half the stalls and closed circuit TV monitors were installed to watch what is arguably the most famous scene in Shakespeare. (The reactions of the patrons are recorded.) The height of *The Dream* set, fifteen foot, was a known factor – the production had already played for a year in Stratford and six weeks on Broadway. The problem of the Aldwych sightlines was also known.

Peter took one look and said: 'Slice three feet off the whole set'.

Walls, walkways and all.

Why had he allowed it to happen? The set could have been adapted in the workshops at little cost and without taking away precious stage time. I suspect it was one of Peter's gambits for rallying everybody behind a production, creating a crisis that all were involved in solving. Whatever the motive, it worked. The entire work force was galvanised into action sawing, hacking and welding. Excitement was back in the air. It took nine hours to complete. Brook was unperturbed.

I was reminded of this as I watched the first preview of *The Mayor of Zalamea* in the Cottesloe Theatre in 1984. The feeling had been growing on me all through the technical period that the play was only being half released; that the set was hindering a good piece of work from emerging. Ironically, this was the only occasion that I had had the use of an original set from the very first day of rehearsal. It was designed by Stephanie Howard, a series of zip-up towers and walkways, black, set on a white floor. It had been built for me at the back of the Lyttleton stage and we had worked solidly on it for six weeks. The costumes were stunning, blood red, amber and ochre, big felt hats, worn, lived in, dusty, dirty. I had an urge to see them all on their own, unencumbered by the structure, against the white floor. I asked Peter Hall to come and look at the second preview and then asked his opinion about the set. 'You're right' he said 'what are you going to do about it?' 'I'm going to cut it' I said.

'Can you?'

'Yes'.

'You're a very merry fellow'.

I talked to Stephanie, who was willing. She too, liked the costumes and was not overly fond of the set. I called the company together and put it to them, expecting opposition. There was a stunned silence. They had worked on this structure solidly now for seven weeks.

It was Thursday. We were to open the following Tuesday. Then Dan Massey spoke. 'You have such a feeling for this play, Mike, that if you think this is the right decision, we're completely behind you'. Euphoria took over, then schizophrenia. The hardest physical task in changing over in such a short time from a production that had been conceived on levels and staircases, to one on a bare stage, was to re-choreograph the fights. Malcolm Ranson nearly turned a cartwheel when I told him. All that Errol Flynn work out of the window, or rather, off the scaffolding. No more heroic leaps from the platforms, falls down the stairs. Moreover, although we were rehearsing on the flat, preparing the bare stage version, the next two performances had to take place on the original set. We were working on one kind of production during the day, performing another in the evening.

Saturday waved goodbye to the structure. On Monday, for the first time, we performed the new bare-stage version. The transformation had been magical. The lighting picked out the blood red colours of the costumes starkly against the white floor and the black back-ground, evoking the passion and heat of Spain. The fights spilled over the Cottesloe stage in a wave of movement. A towering central performance from Michael Bryant. This was the first time the play had been performed in Britain ever. Three hundred years old, it qualified for an award in the 'new plays' section. Instinct and decision had been right.

* * *

Brook put me in charge of the re-rehearsals for the New York run. I had three weeks on my own with the replacements of Terry Taplin as Lysander, Philip Manikum as Starveling and Patrick Stewart as Snout. Once again Peter arrived only two days before we opened. I have often been in the situation as director, of entrusting my assistant with rehearsals for a revival or transfer; if some things do go a little astray, it takes a very short space of time to rectify them. If the assistant has been properly involved in the rehearsal/devising process, then they will have a fundamental grasp of the thrust of the production and the work will be invaluable a) for preparing the actors, b) giving the assistant a proper sense of responsibility. Nothing promotes the confidence of an assistant more than this demonstration of implicit trust, and nothing will give him/her more status in the actors' eyes. Given half a chance, many actors, particularly senior ones, will treat the assistant like shit ('I'm talking to the engine driver, not the toerag') refusing to discuss or act on notes taken of their performance and insisting on altering a scene only on the say-so of the director. As do some young directors.

I directed a world premiere by Alan Byrne of *Please Smash the Glass Gently* at the Eblana Theatre (in the Bus Station) for the Dublin Theatre Festival in 1967. The leading role was taken by Seamus Ford, a sixty-five year old Radio Eirann repertory player, appearing on stage for the first time in twenty years. He addressed me in the third person, through an inter-mediary, appeared not to hear anything I said, and on being asked to sit at the table as indicated in the stage directions, said querulously, in a voice trembling with age and indignation – 'No young whippersnapper upstart director tells me where to go on stage – I go where I like'. And he did just that, over chairs, sofas, lying on his back, climbed out the window, up-staged all and sundry. I was powerless. We all cheered when he finally walked out. Then walked back in again saying – 'I will give my all for the sake of my art'. They don't come any better than that, folks.

Actors like this can make an assistant's life a misery, particularly on a long tour, by refusing to attend re-rehearsals, understudy calls or acknowledge that there is a fault that has to be put right. It creates great difficulties for the assistant if one has to call a company together and tell them, nay insist, that the assistant is the designated deputy, the director's mouth piece, and in his or her absence has full authority to take charge of the production. Is it any wonder that, in these circumstances, an assistant director often forms alliances with younger members of the company, those playing small parts, straight out of drama school, walking under-studies etcetera. The weak and the resentful join forces in a show of solidarity. Occasionally this can be productive, in as much as small projects can be devised to insulate each other from the worst excesses of tour fatigue or long-run-itis. In fact it is essential for any assistant or young actor's sanity to occupy themselves in this way, to keep the wits sharp, exercise the creative muscles, keep in training. On the other hand, some director/assistant partnerships develop into powerful creative teams – Trevor Nunn and John Caird . . .

* * *

Peter invited me to accompany him on visits to every loft, cellar, cafe, studio theatre in and around New York in an insatiable desire to find and experience something new. We avoided traditional theatres like the plague. He often went back stage to question the actors or director, never introducing himself and never assuming that they knew him. Merely curious. Many a theatre practitioner would have probably kicked themselves had they known they had missed the chance to question for themselves one of the great masters of the last sixty years. Maybe that's what Brooky intended . . .

In one such loft, The Performance Garage, founded by alternative scene guru Richard Schechner, we attended a performance of a devised piece, *The Commune*, by his company The Performance Group. The audience sat on a series of diving boards set at different levels overlooking the action, which consisted of some twenty odd (some very odd) naked bodies cavorting and chanting below. Surviving a hail of anti-bourgeois missiles in the shape of jelly-babies that were intermittently and inexplicably launched at us in an attempt to dislodge us from our diving boards, the company then struck a series of contorted poses. One extremely hirsute, thin, naked man upended himself in a head-stand lotus position immediately underneath my board and I found myself staring down at the hairiest, encrusted . . . I know it's distasteful but stay with it 'cos there is a pay off. For five minutes I had to find alternative areas of focus while struggling to avoid my gaze being drawn back to one of the most off-putting images it has ever been my luck to experience in the theatre.

When I got back to London I bought the Sunday papers and turning to the Arts section in *The Sunday Times* found a two page round-up of the alternative theatre scene in New York. And there in the middle was a photograph of the Joseph Schechner production. And there in the middle of that photograph was an hairy man. And that hairy man was my man. And I laughed and I laughed and I laughed.

'What's up?' asked my wife.

'What's up? I bet I'm the only person in Britain reading this article who knows down to the last pimple what that guy's arsehole looks like'. And Peter Brook of course.

It was also while in New York that one of the even more bizarre episodes of my life as an assistant occurred. Peter and myself (nobody else) were invited to a reception given for us (Peter that is) by Vladimir Nabakov, the Russian exile novelist of (the then) *Lolita* fame. We were staying at the Chelsea Hotel, then (as now, if more self-consciously,) the hub of downtown New York bohemian life. Peter and I arranged to meet in the foyer, dressed 'informally'. I wore sneakers, jeans, a red polo-neck jumper and a jeans jacket. When I got downstairs, to my horror, Peter was dressed exactly the same. We are both about the same height and we looked like Tweedle-dum and Tweedle-dee. It was as if I were consciously aping the master – the way to be a good director is to copy the manner of dressing – the assistant as clone. The assistant as prat.

Peter laughed. 'Heh, heh, heh!' I turned to go back upstairs – 'I'll put something else on'.

'No don't do that, the Americans will appreciate it, it's what they expect'. Unconvinced, feeling extremely foolish, I made my way with him to Nabakov's. It was a wonderful penthouse, overlooking the whole of New York – and the whole of New York gliterati were there – in various states of evening undress. Those that couldn't get round or within ten feet of the dumpy red polo-necked figure of Peter at one end of the room stage-left, got the dumpy red polo-necked figure of his assistant at the other, stage-right. If they couldn't have Peter, they could have the next best thing. One small bespectacled figure, who had been hovering on the outskirts for half an hour while I pompously expounded my views on life and art as seen through the eyes of Peter Brook, finally found enough courage to speak.

'Would Peter Brook mind if I came to Paris to watch some rehearsals?'

'No, I'm sure he wouldn't, he has observers all the time', I answered glibly assuming the importance of a private secretary.

'I wouldn't be any trouble, I'd just sit there at the back and listen.'

'I'm sure that would be possible.'

'Oh, it would be such an honour. How do I go about it?'

'The best thing to do is to give me your address.'

'Oh, you mean he'll write to *me*?'

'Well, I don't know if he'll write personally but . . .'

'Look, I'll give you my telephone number.' He pulled out a small diary

'This one will get me in New York and this one in Los Angeles, but I may not be at either, so this is my ranch'.

I took the piece of paper

'That's *ok*, I'm sure we'll find you, Mr . . .' I looked down 'Arthur Penn?!'

I started gibbering like an idiot, my loftiness punctured with the rapidity of a burst tyre. Arthur Penn, my cinematic hero, director of *The Miracle Worker*, *The Left Handed Gun*, *Bonnie and Clyde*. Humbly begging to come and sit quietly at the back of Brookie's rehearsals. I became the pupil again, idiotically pouring out naïve questions about his work, as others had previously been plying me. 'What's it like to work with Faye Dunaway? Paul Newman? Warren Beatty?' This clone felt a right clown.

I still have three personal telephone numbers and addresses in Arthur Penn's handwriting, written on the torn out page of a diary for 1972 on the day of 14th February.

The experience of *The Dream* had made my decision to begin again at the age of thirty as an assistant director at Stratford, worthwhile. It made me realise that, despite the offer of a further year and the carrot of a production of *Miss Julie* with Donal McCann and Helen Mirren at The Place (Robin Phillips did it), I had to get out and put my ideas into practice. Trevor called me into his office at the end and asked me if he thought I had worked hard that year. Sometimes, I said. He looked at me with those unblinking eyes of his, then nodded. Sometimes . . .

6

Carrying the Can

It is strange to hear people talk about a director's culture in Britain. The person on the ground floor of the privatised Clapham Badger Line coach service would be hard pushed to name you any director of theatre in this country. Maybe Sir Peter Hall for the number of his wives or Dr. Jonathan Miller for the number of his TV appearances. Unlike our continental European counterparts where the director often assumes the status of a god, we have always believed the actor to be paramount and, since Elizabethan times, have accorded the actor the status and central position on our stages that the director occupies, for example, in central Europe. So insignificant is the director's position in the hierarchy of writer/designer/choreographer/lighting designer /director that, while all the others have copyright on their works, a director does not. They don't know what a director does you see. I mean, what do directors actually do? Sort of organise, don't they? Tell actors where to stand, that sort of thing.

Most Thesauri give a list of adjectival equivalents that describe a megalomaniac.

'Director: The person responsible for supervising the performance of a play (film) of an actor.' The term director as such is a fairly recent development in theatrical history. Until the mid-nineteenth century the stage manager was mainly responsible for hiring actors and organising the making of sets and costumes, while the leading actor polished up the production at one or two rehearsals, mainly to see that nothing interfered with his own role. In the 1820's directors (or producers as they were then called) began to be credited with the staging of pantomime and entertainments and by the 1870's it was common to give the 'director' a credit on the programme, though he would always have some other connection to the play – writer, leading actor, stage manager. From the 1900's the term producer began to be more widely used (Gordon Craig still writes in *The Art of the Theatre* of the 'stage manager') but was finally replaced by the 'director' shortly after Second World War.

But the real rise and rise of the director begins with the advent of Jung, Freud, Hebert, Adler – all the lads – who contributed to the development of naturalism in the theatre, which found its apotheosis in Stanislavski, whose basic tenets still form, over a hundred years later, the backbone of contemporary theatre writing, acting and directing, particularly that for television.

Charles Marowitz 'There are two ways to begin work. Either one says: this is the play and these are the actors and let's see what spontaneous combustion produces or: this is the play, this is the Idea, let us try to get these actors to realise the Idea. I think the spontaneous combustion route is the haven of the talentless director, the guy who really believes that casting will carry the day. I can't conceive of approaching a play without a handle full of ideas, but that is not to say that an arbitrary or imposed idea will not reduce all to smithereens . . . Mr X is too nice and genial to be a ball-busting Metteur-en-Scene with an over-weaning idea of the whole. This really is a British weakness. The Germans, for instance, do not suffer from it at all. They always come forearmed with conceptions galore and occasionally produce some interesting work. I don't think 'concept' productions are what's wrong; but muddily 'concept' productions . . . and it's always possible to 'talk a great show' if you're from Oxbridge and have been led to believe that ideas can have a life of their own and can animate plays willy nilly'.

The objection to the 'ball-busting metteur-en-scene' is that he or she either reduces the actors to ciphers, puppets and gibbering wrecks, or they surround themselves with simpering side-kicks who rubber-stamp every whim and wish. Ninagawa's *Peer Gynt* and Yuri Lubymov's Taganga Theatre production of *Hamlet*, both a l'Anglaise, were testimony to British actors fighting a losing battle with a revolving globe or a mobile curtain. Good performers whose balls were busted.

What then does a modern director do? Pass. There is no formula for conceiving and rehearsing a project. Each director or group employs a different technique and, with individual directors, there are often vastly differing methods, depending on circumstances. Most directors attempt to arrive at a point where their work method is a constant and ongoing exploration of theatre practice, the approach being subject to the same rules and conditions each time. The luxury that small groups possess, working outside the mainstream and often founded on a set of burning principles, is that they can choose their methods and are answerable only to themselves. Conventional buildings and spaces often limit the freedom to choose, dictate work methods and deadlines, and impose formal restrictions that 'poor' theatre is unconcerned with. Hence the move away from conventional spaces to work that is sometimes more akin to an art installation project, aka the National Theatres of Wales and Scotland: projects on beaches, up trees, under railway arches, in disused mine shafts, ferrying audiences around towns in taxis, buses, performing for eight people in a caravan, travelling the rooms of a country house, blurring the distinction between the various art forms. Simultaneous action, dialogue and participation of the spectators. Only occasionally does a director or a group transcend these prescribed limitations of traditional spaces and bring a whiff of guerrilla gunshot from the outside.

I am often asked how long I like to rehearse. How long is a piece of string. A one-person show can take six months, a Shakespeare two weeks. Some productions involve collaborative research, reading, interviews, teach-ins, location work, role immersion – others involve reading the text and then getting on with it, the actor sometimes carrying the text until the last possible moment, an umbilical life-belt thrown around insecurity. This often accounts for a radical change in the strength of a performance during the course of a run of a play, the difference not entirely accounted for by the input of the audience. The rehearsal process is usually too short, the actor's familiarity with the role too shallow, the know-ledge of the text too insecure, the technical period too frenetic to allow the performance to acquire depth and security. In Germany, in Eastern Europe, performances deepen. In Britain they change. A director returning to a production after a short absence to remove the 'improvements' is often merely attempting to re-establish what, in fact, was only a fragile truce called at the moment of critical unveiling between himself, the actors, the text and the audience.

This process of exploration during the course of live performance is natural and inevitable. The danger arises when the ground-work has not been thorough enough, and the corral is not strong enough to contain the team of wild horses which now stampedes in every direction with the director straining to hold a dozen reins in each hand. The hardest thing of all for a director to achieve is a communal objective. This is why many directors (particularly in continental Europe) find it easier to strait-jacket a concept, tying their actors to a particular style and method.

It is this that gives rise to the term 'director's theatre' a form that, despite occasional maverick examples, is relatively unknown in this country. Most people would be hard pushed to put a director's name to a piece of work in Britain, so 'style-less' is the product. Is this a virtue? Certainly the demagogic, hierarchical approach of authoritarian directors is one which the liberal shrinking violet of the British psyche shies away from, and yet all those directors whose work demands serious attention proceed from a clearly defined set of primal and personal objectives which usually demand the total submersion of the individual in the waters of the director's will.

Does it mean, then, that British mainstream directors lack seriousness as defined by theory and practice? Is there a discernible philosophy behind the work of Adrian Noble, Trevor Nunn, Declan Donnellan, Nicholas Hytner, Peter Hall, Deborah Warner, Matthew Warchus, Sam Mendes, Katie Mitchell, Richard Eyre, Terry Hands, Phyllida Lloyd, Howard Davies *et al*? Mostly the reputations are founded on Shakespeare and yet one would be hard pressed to say that any of the above has revitalised our perception of that playwright – Peter Hall in the 60s maybe in founding the ensemble style of the RSC. Their productions are mainly interchangeable and, given a nod towards changing theatrical conventions, well in the mould of cultural conformity and the upholding of traditional views. There are few of whom it can be said they have left even a clean footprint in the sand, or have a serious performance art that transcends naturalistic praxis. What else is the theatre of Mike Leigh, other than the obverse side of Katie Mitchell's? Given that, in Britain at least, Ibsen is not the object of de-construction and given that most British theatre has managed to avoid post-modernism, (I count myself among those who conform) what else can a director do other than create in the most naturalistic detail, the minutiae of 'life' in art? The longer the rehearsal process, the more realistic (and obsessive) these details become. The British temperament is ideally suited to the Nordic theatre of Ibsen and Strindberg and the controlled passion of Chekhov, and the object quickly becomes to have the best 'acted' production. The direction is good because it is 'unobtrusive' and does not 'impose' itself on the text. In other words, good directors should neither be seen nor heard.

Some directors improvise right up to the moment of performance, others dictate moves, line readings, emphases and pauses from the word go. Some allow freedom up to the halfway mark and then shut up shop. Others create a quick framework and then relax. Some plough methodically on with a combination of literary and psychological analysis, allied to a 'I don't think I'd do that at that moment' approach. Such descriptions of methods of directing reveal nothing of the iceberg. An advertised concept, as revealed in articles, interviews, programme notes, may never materialise, the reasons being long since buried on the floor of the rehearsal room along with the broken bits of a failed model box of the set.

The thing is that each production has a secret history before it ever hits the streets, and 'if the final result is a breathtaking demonstration of a director's signature the point to remember is that whatever the clarity of the work, it has been dredged through a muddy and resistant element to get there' (says Irving Wardle).

In order for a production to be understood, the concept which inspires it must be grasped by the audience. This concept must be made visible in some way or other; if the spectators do not perceive it, they will get the impression that they have not seen a production, that they have winessed things happening without any coherence or unity. On the other hand, if a concept is made too visible because it is too simplistic, rudimentary or over-obvious, the production will be dismissed as facile or shallow, giving the impression that once the initial idea has been under-stood, all the rest will follow as a matter of course. Many British directors, unlike their continental counterparts, protest that they do not try to impose a reading of the text. 'I serve the playwright, not myself', although the new wave of Rupert Goold, Emma Rice, Melly Still, Mariane Elliot, Josie Rourke, Tim Supple etc., is possibly changing that perception. (Note that there are four female directors in that latter group.)

Carrying the Can

This attitude of non-interpretation is often demanded by the authors themselves: according to them, directors should let the texts speak for themselves. Thus Heiner Mueller praises American Bob Wilson's direction saying 'He never interprets a text, contrary to the practice of directors in Europe.' This is patently nonsense – naïve and dishonest. A director does not try to preserve textual ambiguities, neither does the actor. It is an impossibility. Direction and acting are the exact opposite of neutrality and there is no way in which a text may speak for itself: it's a contradiction in terms, for one cannot avoid interpretation. A text has to be made to speak, and as soon as an actor opens their mouth what issues forth is an interpretation. Simply because a director denies that a production has any concept, does not mean that this concept is suddenly going to disappear as if by magic. The distinction made between a performance as an objective abstract and a production as a concrete experience enables us to assess the intention of a production and our perception of it. Indeed, a production only exists when it is received and re-constructed by an audience, each member interpreting individually the work of an artistic team, even if it does not always understand the way in which the production has been put together. The latter should be the job of the critic (I am being wildly optimistic in this assumption).

Frank Hauser – the then Artistic Director of the Oxford Playhouse – once said to me – 'As you get older, you learn to just leave it all to the actors'. In the days of 'homework' I used to prepare my productions with a set of drafts and a series of diagrams that resembled nothing so much as a demented game of noughts and crosses. It was not until the fringe revolution, sparked off by the American experimental invasion, that the opportunity came to dispense with these production crutches and enter into a free-fall experience in conjunction with a group of actors. The legacy of my homework, however, is still there. I learned the rules in order to break them. 'Blocking' (staging) became a sleight of hand, something that I could do at a moment's notice when all else failed. It gave me the confidence to work spatially with large numbers of people on a bare stage, secure in the knowledge of how to place people in apposition to each other, yet still able to experiment and improvise. The danger is to try and abandon the rules altogether, (an impossibility anyway in any form of conventional space where characters have to get on and off the stage in some semblance of order).

The directing technique I have finally arrived at is one of the lasso. I come to a piece of work armed with a strong framework (yes, the homework these days is often a trunk load of books). But I try to let the process be organic, spontaneous. There are many routes from A to B, detours, zigzags, and a whole heap of blind alleys. The important thing is to know the journey – the starting point A, the finishing point B. Of course, sometimes I end up at C. This either spells disaster (mostly) or in the course of rehearsals, I have discovered personally, or we have arrived at the conclusion collectively, that there is something in the play that I or we had not recognised before and have altered course accordingly. This occurs particularly when the rehearsal period is open ended, a virtually extinct species, or I have come to a project with a blank sheet, employing the ultimate, democratic, organic process of theatre through discovery. Exciting but dangerous . . . (I think an example was sighted somewhere around 1974 but rumours of later appearances are unsubstantiated).

Around this journey from A to B, I throw the lasso, the framework, metaphorically mixing. The actors are given great freedom to explore, to investigate, voice opinions, as the search for the centre of the play progresses. Gradually, I pull the lasso tighter until there is no more movement possible. Then I release it on to stage.

Time permitting, if we are working on a text-based play, I will have started by going through the text slowly, debating every line, every meaning and possible variation within the given framework I've presented as a view of the piece. If working on a new play or an adaptation this will often involve rewriting, both at this stage and in rehearsal – writer willing, if present. There are those playwrights notorious for refusing to have a word changed, thus denying that mysterious process whereby the meaning of a whole scene is altered by an actor's inflexion.

It is important for me that all the company are involved in this process, that no one is excluded. There cannot be an abdication of responsibility either by myself or by the actor for what happens on stage. This can only be achieved by group discussion, throwing ideas into the middle of the ring, kicking them around, saying 'crap' to some, 'terrific' to others, one person producing a brilliant idea, another an awful one. Ideas are a hundred a penny. My function is to supply a platform on which everyone can build the edifice. Without discussion, collaboration and proper involvement, no actor can have their heart in what happens. The excuse 'I'm only doing this, because that is what the director wanted' should never pertain. For example, one should not be able to look at the edges of a Shakespeare production and see nothing there, no generalised servants or messengers. Often what these 'peripheral' characters say is of vital importance. It is a truism to say that there are no small parts, only small actors – but it is true. Rehearsal should be the verification of that truth.

I am not making any particular claims for this method for this is the technique of many directors, yet whenever there is not enough discussion or involvement, it leads to the rehearsal of scenes in isolation and invariably the left hand never knows what the right is doing. Actors should be encouraged to be present at all times. Peter Zadek even locked the doors, providing food and drink for the whole company who remained in the same room all day, even if the majority were not used. That's taking things a bit too far. As one of the great improvisers of the European stage –

as loose as Stein is anal – Zadek started his life in Wales, doing weekly rep in Pontypridd and Swansea. You only have to see his close-in work to know that – however wild and undisciplined his more extravagant pageants became.

Actors should be encouraged to follow the course of a performance, to watch and listen to their fellow artists. This way the rhythm of a performance can be properly sustained. If an actor has only one appearance and late in the play at that, it is vital that the tempo of the scenes prior to that appearance has been absorbed. I have fought with actors over this. I have often witnessed a performance skidding to a halt, the tempo and rhythm having altered drastically as a result of a new character arriving on stage and being totally unaware of what the other actors have set up in the preceding scenes. In an effort to combat this, my 'wrap-around' for a production has often been to have the actors on stage throughout the whole of the performance. This is one way at least to combat the cards and i-phone backstage.

The time spent combing and analysing the text at the beginning of rehearsals is time well spent; piecing the jigsaw together in the correct manner, binding every single phrase to ensure that the same story is being told by each and every member of the cast. This encourages the production to flourish in other directions; for example, it will allow the visual side to compliment and reinforce the story instead of fighting it. I often leave decisions as to what goes on the set in the way of props and dressing to the rehearsal process. It can drive designers and workshops mad, when, as is inevitable, requests for large items suddenly arrive at short notice.

But it is worth it. In this age of mechanically, hydraulically, technocratically operated productions, it is one small gesture in the direction of theatre as an organic process. The only way to change the situation is to run your own theatre, and make your own rules or operate a company in a warehouse where you can put a low price on scenic decoration, and work with only minimal props and costumes that can be designed alongside rehearsals.

Theatre practice in England has moved a long way from the days of weekly-rep 'blocking' but every aspiring director should try it as an exercise, going through the text working out all the moves – even if it all goes out the window when you are confronted with real life, flesh and blood actors, who won't behave as your noughts, crosses and black and white drafts did.

There is no real answer to the question 'What is good direction' or what constitutes directors' theatre. The direction may be obtrusive to the point of being breathtakingly spectacular or a fatal distraction. The imprint of a director may be there or not, overt or secreted. But it is there. The point to remember is that, whatever the result, cohesion or shambles, the performance has been 'directed'. Nothing arrives on stage of its own volition. Someone carries the can.

7

The Street

The street is where theatre begins. It started there, it continues to be there. . . . When the wall came down, what happened in the streets of Berlin was far more exciting than what was happening in the theatre. The Troubles in Ireland, Iraq, The Arab Spring – Revolution and war may be fuelled by intellect, but when the real action starts, no one wants to see yet another version of *Hedda Gabler* or *Time and the Conways*. Or do they?

In the ghetto of Vilnya it was theatre that united the spirit of Jewish resistance, and in the aftermath of violent upheavals art often nourishes the conscience – pointing an accusing finger at the mistakes, encouraging the successes, helping heal the open wounds of angst, showing the way forward. In America the McCarthy witch-hunts and Vietnam produced a wave of artistic anger. Alternative groups sprang up to articulate a new mood of protest, embracing civil rights, racial equality and a wave of left wing thinking in a country dominated by the hard right. For the mainstream, Arthur Miller and Brecht in exile, carried the torch.

But the real action was in the street and in the warehouses. Post-beat and pre-hippy groups such as The Living Theatre, La Mama, The Bread and Puppet Theatre, The Paper Bag Players, The Open Theatre, joined forces to become the most potent and influential force in Western theatre this side of the Second World War. The productions were overtly political, so much so that The

The Street

Living Theatre under the artistic direction of Julien Beck and Judith Melina, after being busted, arrested and closed down on a number of occasions, had to flee into exile as did many other leading figures. It became fashionable to accuse those that settled in Europe of draft dodging, but historically those groups and their creators gave birth to the post war European fringe movement. We owe the Traverse in Edinburgh to Jim Haynes, the Open Space to Charles Marowitz, Inter-Action to Ed Berman and Nancy Meckler (an early female leader and who is still a directing force in this country) formed one of the most exciting groups of the sixties and seventies – the Freehold. The streets were alive with jugglers, fire eaters, escapologists. The Ken Campbell Road Show began to roll. It was timely. It was not simply the optimistic mood of the sixties, the feeling that the dark days were behind and the brave new world was just around the corner; there was a genuine trans-continental theatre movement that swept aside barriers of gender, race and religion and united a whole generation in its ideology of equality and change. And it was born on the wings of an American regime of repression. There was something to protest about.

I rode a Greyhound bus from Knoxville Tennessee to Birmingham Alabama in the summer of 1961 with a group of Freedom Riders, four white and one black. Bus stations had segregated toilets and eateries, buses ditto. Some buses were all white. The Riders were attempting to bust open the policy. They began with an impromptu show in the bus station, performed an anti racial parable on the bus based on the experiences of a nineteenth century plantation slave, during the journey, and engaged in active debate with the passengers, eliciting violent responses from many, some of whom left the bus at various points en route. In Birmingham they tried to take the black actor in the group into the bus station cafe with them, supported by members of the public who were sympathetic or who had been converted

71

en route. A fight broke out. Some were arrested. I found myself in jail for the night and allowed out the next morning only because of my British passport. I don't know what happened to the others. I hitch-hiked on to New Orleans. On the way, I passed a huge crowd surrounding a burning bus. Many were singing and dancing and waving flags. A white stilt-walker was carrying a small black child in his arms.

* * *

During the miners strike in '84 many theatre groups lent their support in the streets and at the pit-heads, to the miners' cause. The RNT produced a piece of work The Garden of England in conjunction with a Kent Mining Community, overtly embracing a political cause. Most of the time, however, protest theatre in this country is marginalised, dismissed contemptuously by the critics as agit-prop. These days of Cameron/Blair-blandness it is hard to get anyone to take radical ideas seriously, whether on the page or the stage. We, the artists, are to blame. We did not take to the streets in force at the point when we should have done. We have allowed our natural base to be eroded. Our debating platform has been taken over by the propagators of market forces; commercial consideration has replaced artistic integrity, the wrapping has become more important than the contents. Two million of us marched against the war in Iraq. Blair said – 'Sorry, I'm going to war anyway'. We said – 'Oh, all right then', and turned round and went home. Why didn't we throw him out on his ear? I'm as guilty as anyone.

Until recently, I always tried to produce at least one piece of street theatre a year. This helped me stay in touch with the fundamentals of story telling. Holding on to an audience in a shopping mall, a park or in a square, is an art in itself. Most people don't have time to dally. Persuading people to stop, getting across a message coupled with entertainment gives you fifteen minutes at most. Cabotinage or commedia. Involve the audience in the action. The crowd stays longer if one of its members has been prevailed upon to contribute. Then it is possible to open up debate. The tradition of political street theatre is strong in the rest of Europe and South America – Boal, Eugenio Barba, Dario Fo – all have raised the involvement of working communities to a high art. Barba's system of 'barter' theatre has had enormous influence. A school lacks library books? The admission charge is one book (or as many as you like). Ditto Boal's Forum theatre, where a community works out the solutions to its problems by making decisions which influence the direction in which the story goes, the audience eventually changing places with the performers to demonstrate what they mean. A rehearsal for change that then brings about the actual change. When a solution to a communal problem has been found it is then put into operation.

A chance visit by Brazilian supremo Ruth Escobar to the Oxford Playhouse in 1969 to see my own musical adaptation of *Le Bourgeois Gentilhomme – The Bootleg Gentleman* – set in the thirties, resulted in an invitation in 1971 to go to San Paolo to direct *Two Gentlemen of Verona – Os Dos Cabelleros di Verona*. The Brazilian actors were terrific, their capacity for improvisation astonishing.

Rehearsals took place in the evening and would go on until one or two in the morning. I tried to change this to accommodate my own rhythm and start earlier in the day, but had to give up. Punctuality was the problem. And relatives of the actors kept disappearing as did, on one occasion, one of the actresses. Without trace. The repressive Brazilian regime was in full swing and many artists were in exile.

One night in a restaurant I was introduced to a director and some of his actors. I didn't catch his name, but picked up that he was the director of the Arena Theatre in Sao Paulo. He didn't say much, but after a few litres of Brazilian beer I was in full naïve flight, laying down the law about political engagement in art from my cosy, white, liberal, British viewpoint. The man got up and left. One of the actors started to explain his theories to me. What's his name again? I asked. Augusto Boal. This meant nothing to me. It was not until many years later that I read Boal's 'The Theatre of the Oppressed', published shortly after my visit, which outlined what it was really like to engage in political theatre in South America. Boal's theories of empowerment of the people to act through a theatrical confrontation of the problems that they face – theatre as a rehearsal for revolution – struck a powerful chord in me. Taken in conjunction with a main plank of The Living Theatre's credo – the release of anger and aggression through audience confrontation, which is then channelled by that audience into direct action – (alongside a bit of Tommy Cooper – 'not like that – like that') – I had got a recipe for theatre.

We sat all through the night, discussing how to use theatre as a catalyst for revolution, (one of the few occasions when such a discussion has had any real meaning for me), and I went straight from the café to rehearsal, enthused and inspired with a passion to change the world through my work.

What? *Os Dos Cabelieros di Verona*?!

I realised my mistake in coming to Brazil to direct a play based on the wrong premise. Never direct a play because (a) you think you should (b) someone says you should (c) you think you can do it better than someone else (d) an actor wants to do it (e) you think you should be able to do it. (If you need the money, forget anything I've said). Always do a play because you want to say something about a facet of life that is obsessing you and, at that moment, a particular play says it better than any other. You must have a burning desire to do a play. No other reason will do. There are always exceptions. You stumble into a brilliant piece of work through having accepted an egotistical challenge or being unable to turn down an offer for fear you will never work again. (This latter paranoia is particularly prevalent.) But for every time you do a good piece of work in this way, there are five that are mediocre or bad.

I was able to do something immediately with 'The Two Gents'. The Outlaws, up to then merely the subject of a vague gesture in the direction of drop-outs, took on a new significance. We immediately re-translated the word to bring it into line with the contemporary meaning of Brazilian exile and improvised a series of torture and terror scenes, two of which found their way into the production, including a Kafkaesque journey through a tangled mesh of rope, accompanied by laser-like strobe lighting. The Brazilian actors are brilliant improvisers, sexually and physically fearless but, of course, anything overtly political ran the risk of imprisonment and torture, hence the disappearances. 'Who hasn't experienced the knock on the door in the middle of the night' says Jan Kott. Unfortunately, British bankers.

My puny effort at a statement, a small chunk in the middle of a minor Shakespeare comedy, wrenching a few unfinished scenes of arcadian exile and anonymous characters (First, Second, Third Outlaw) into a political present, would go unnoticed.

Boal's influence has been enormous if often only indirectly in the creation of the community play/event – investigating a community's cultural roots and very *raison d'être*. Independent visits in 2013 from the New York company the Nature Theatre of Oklahoma and a group of Argentinian actors to the Brighton Festival, exploring life under a dictatorship, demonstrate that the engaged principals of Boal's Theatre of the Oppressed are alive and well – at least in the Americas.

I devised a road show at the Phoenix Theatre Leicester in 1976 to perform in the streets, community centres, hospitals, etc. It was down to Ken Campbell, who died in 2011, a marvellous, original, eccentric man, and an intensely human person, to whom I owe an enormous personal debt. His Ken Campbell Roadshows influenced the way myself and others looked at community and street theatre and many of his stunts I filched for my companies at the Phoenix and the Young Vic. Led by Downton Butler Bates Jim Carter, who taught my children to wire-walk, unicycle, juggle, we trained up a group of circus and street performers, all of us with a passion for rough theatre. The shirt removal trick, where a stooge has his shirt removed from under his coat by gripping the collar and whipping it off in one piece while the man remains otherwise fully dressed remains one of the seminal moments of that particular era of my life. That and the bed of nails, fire blowing, escapology, hammering a nail up the nose, escaping from a sack, decapitation – the usual bundle of tricks.

We built into our fun and jinx for the Phoenix show as much satire and political comment as we could cull from the local and national papers. We asked to be let perform it at Garston Borstal believing that we could make real contact with the boys through our piece of butch, anarchic, anti-authoritarian fun. We were a monster success.

The Warden rang the next day to say the boys were so enthusiastic that they wanted to learn the stunts for themselves and put their own show together, would we be willing to provide actors on a regular basis to do this? We were jubilant. This is what we wanted. Theatre as therapy. Theatre as a means of rehabilitation. Theatre helping people re-adjust to society (I'll beg the question as to how right-wing a sentiment that is. Many people are better off not being anaesthetised and slotted back into a social groove of conformist respectability).

A number of actors duly went out to teach the lads the tricks of the trade. Eight of them got a show together and played it for the rest of the inmates. It was a huge success. The next day the Warden rang again, wildly excited. The boys wanted to perform it outside in the community. They wanted to take it to an old people's home as we at the Phoenix Theatre had done. Better and better. We congratulated ourselves on discharging our proper responsibility, as artists, to the community we were working in.

The Borstal boys were booked into the home. The day arrived of the performance. None of us could go as we were either performing ourselves or rehearsing. The next day the Warden rang for a third time. A hundred old people had been in the Hall. They had waited and waited. The boys had done a bunk out of the back through the toilet window. Seven had been re-captured and one was still on the loose. I like to think that their real escapology act was a complete spur of the moment decision and that somewhere, somehow one of those Leicester boys is teaching other Young Offenders to hammer nails up the nose instead of into somebody's head. As I said, it was all down to Ken Campbell . . .

I shared a port-a-cabin for a week with Ken in downtown LA, one of the funniest weeks of my life, and at the same time deadly serious. We were there to write a musical version of *Baba the Elephant* and look at possible disused film studios in which to stage it with real elephants. These belonged to David Balding Jenks, founder of the Big Apple Circus, who had commissioned the piece. The music for *Baba* was originally composed by Ray Davies of The Kinks, but he dropped out and one of the reasons we were in LA was to collaborate with Randy Newman, with whom we worked for a couple of days. The project eventually collapsed as the French estate withdrew the rights.

I once went round to Ken's eccentric shack in Hackney Marshes for the evening.

"Ere Mike', he said, in that East London nasal voice of his, 'I'm getting married. A Phillipino girl. I got her from an ad. We've been writing to each other for a month. Look.' And he pulled a sheaf of dog-eared letters and a thumbed photo out from under his coat.

'She's coming over next week for a month on approval. If it doesn't work out you send her back and get another one. You can marry as many times as you like in Manila.'

'But not here Ken', I said.

'Well I'll probably keep her then. ''Ere, look at this, she's lovely, the future Mrs. Campbell, except that I've a mind to take her name – Ken Vatutu; sounds better dunn it?'

I ran into him several times on Sark where he used to holiday. Each time there was some fantastical interterrestial theory on which he was working. The last time I saw him was at the Sherman Theatre, Cardiff a few years ago. I walked into his dressing room and he immediately launched into a treatise on relativity and human beings comprised simply of light as if the intervening years hadn't happened. Only Ken could persuade a couple in Liverpool to let him knock a huge hole in their living room wall so that honoured guests from the National Theatre could sit on their sofa and watch a performance through the wall of *Illuminatus* being performed in the cafe next door, served cups of tea through the night by the lady of the house. Ken Campbell. Lord of Misrule.

Unless theatre has contact with the street, it has no life blood. It has no balls. There is an umbilical cord that connects the two things – the gutter and the guru. Attempts to eradicate the former from our conformist stages will always fail. Feed the body an unbalanced diet and it will break out in boils.

The theatre of niceness is the norm. 'Blasted' is buried beneath a deluge of middle-class abuse. 'Nice' people don't write plays like that, particularly young girls. 'Nice' people don't write plays where people bugger each other, castrate each other, eat dead babies. 'Nice' people say on Radio Five Live (I heard it) – 'Welcome to Auschwitz'. We are rightly shocked at the atrocities committed in Libya, Syria, Rawanda, Afghanistan, and Iraq. What happens in the street is nasty, ugly, dirty. It is time we got a bit of that dirt back under our nails.

8

Travelling Man

Oh the joys of touring. 'I'm a freeborn man of the travelling people . . .' I used to strum it on my guitar. 'Out on Runway Number 9, Big 707 ready to go' . . . John Denver where are you now? I'm a Sagittarian. It would appear that we're restless free spirits. Seven league boots, wanderlust has us in its grip. Well, have you ever got to the point where you hear yourself saying at the top of your voice in a crowded restaurant – 'Oh god. I've got to go to Tokyo for the weekend!' To my infinite shame, I have. Pretentious wanker. You should be so lucky, Bogdanov. We jet setters forget that a lot of the populace might think it a bit of a wheeze to pop over to Japan on a forty-eight hour freebie. But working globally exacts its toll. It is finally no fun sitting sandwiched between a snoring Sumo and a teething child for eighteen hours to arrive ten hours ahead of yourself. What fun is there in flying half way round the world to stay in a Holiday Inn look-alike, straight off the plane into meetings, get smashed in the same anonymous hotel bar, fly back again, ten hours behind, lose a week's sleep and feel like shit? No fun at all.

Touring is not for the faint hearted; idealistic it may be, glamorous it ain't. Even at the sharp end, the constant hassle at the airports drives you crazy. The waiting, the waiting . . .

. . . Sometimes, if you're really lucky you can hit the jackpot and pack every possible disaster into one trip. 'The connection to

Karachi, sir, – sorry, it's just left, the next flight is on Saturday. It would appear that your baggage has turned up in Dallas, you should get it within the week. We did tell you that the hotel didn't have a reservation in the name of Bogdanov. I'm afraid there's nothing we can do about you being next to the air conditioning and above the disco. You did say anything would do and Fakir's use prayer mats to sleep on without any problem. No, the room hasn't been paid for by your firm and we can accept no responsibility for your food poisoning. The doctor's bill is £250 – we don't take cards'.

On a visit to Toronto, I stayed at an hotel that is only rivalled in my experience by the one I inadvertently stayed in outside Coventry (England, not Wisconsin). The doorknob came off in my hand, the door fell from the wardrobe, the basin was cracked and the water ran onto my shoes. The bed was at an angle, with one leg missing, and, unless you think there is nothing with which to cap this, when I sat on the toilet it fell over. I moved. Gino Empery, the Royal Alexandra Theatre press officer, wearing the most wonderful wig I had ever seen, fixed me up with a suite. Sublime to the ridiculous. It was almost a hundred metres end to end. Take a tram to the phone.

The Germans sit carved in stone, immobile for five hours and then cheer wildly for twenty minutes. The Japanese ditto and applaud for twenty seconds. The Irish talk to each other and tell each other the story – 'Did you hear what yer man said?!' The French ask each other the story – '*Qu'est que c'est, cette connerie?!*' The Indians walk in and out, the Americans walk out. The Greeks can't hear because they sit too far away – (it's a myth that a whisper can be heard at Epidaurus 100m back), the Americans can't hear because they're talking too much 'Waddee say?' The Africans don't understand because they don't speak the language, but they listen. The Americans don't understand because they do speak the language but don't listen. 'Waddee say again?!' The

Travelling Man

Australians spend their time trying to work out if they should shout 'Bravo' or 'Pommy bastards'. The Finns listen respectfully and enthusiastically illustrate the sound of one hand clapping. The Chinese remain inscrutably baffled, a fixed smile on their faces (cf. the Koreans, the Japanese, the Malayans). The East Germans (we're talking pre-Wall here) gave you the hardest time of your life ideologically. The Americans don't want to know about that socialist shit. 'Whaas that ee said?' The Russians understand, even if they don't. The French don't, even if they do. And where do the English fit into all this? Taking a cross section of bourgeois theatre audiences around the world, and measured on a scale of fidgeting, coughing, looking around, reading the programme, whispering, murmuring, eating, forgetting to turn off bleepers, alarms, mobiles, the average level of British concentration is the pits. It must be the problem of all the hobbies and habits, games and individual pursuits we go in for. The English audience always gives the impression that it could be doing something better with its time, illustrated by the one luke-warm round of applause that follows a performance, in the course of which some are already leaving and others are busy putting on their coats, gloves, scarves. The actors collude in this; shuffling furtively back onto stage, to give one hasty, embarrassed dip of the cranium, an apology for what passes for a bow, before stampeding *en masse* to the nearest exit off stage, irrespective of how small or inconvenient that exit may be. Unlike the Germans, the Russians, the Poles, the Americans, for whom as long as there's a clap there's a bow.

Given the variety of linguistic problems that performing abroad in English produces, there is no way of altering your performance to suit different cultures. It is no use speaking louder, slower, addressing more of the text out front – the show will have exactly the same psychological effect on an audience of Afghans as it does Liverpudlians; it will be merely louder, slower, more out front. . . . The same applies to directing. An attempt to graft on your political view of an alien culture on the basis of some few weeks acquaintance, is not merely foolhardy, it is arrogant. Only after working in Germany for three years with constant exposure to the politics and culture of the country, and of Hamburg in particular, did I feel that it might be possible to direct a new play by Claus Pohl; but then only on the assurance that he would be by my side night and day. A director has to draw on his or her own culture and background to make social and political statements. For someone like myself, imbued with Welsh and Irish culture, coupled with Kiev/North-West Middlesex-Tropic-of-Ruislip – this means the labour background of my Welsh working-class mother and the Marxism/humanism of my Russian intellectual father, shot through with a good dollop of the Piccadilly and Metropolitan Lines change at Rayners Lane.

The Young Vic Theatre was guesting in Germany with *Hamlet* and *Rosenkranz and Guildernstern Are Dead*. On a dark November morning in Nant-y-Llys, my house up on the edge of the Mynydd Epynt in Breconshire, I awoke at 5 am. It was bucketing down. I donned waterproofs and Wellingtons, gabbed a torch and staggered out into the pitch-black of Niagara Falls.

I opened the shed door, picked up the overfull Elsan with both hands and, spade under arm and torch under chin, squelched my way across the pitch-black darkness of the yard and up into the field, shit and piss slopping over boot and troos.

Laying the torch on the ground, in the sheeting rain, I dug a hole in the boggy ground, poured in the faeces of the Elsan and covered the lot with sodden sods of turf, poo and piss oozing everywhere.

I drowned-ratted my way to the tap on the yard and washed the crap off my boots, put the Elsan and spade back in the shed, stripped off my sopping clothes and changed into shirt and suit, jumped in the car, bumped the mile down the track, drove to Heathrow, got on the plane and at 6 o'clock that evening was sitting in the bar of the Duesseldorf Hilton, surrounded by sleek executives, chic Euro-chicks, businessmen and bankers and for all I know the Bundeskanzler himself. I started to laugh.

And I laughed and I laughed and I laughed.

'What's up?', asked Chris Barnes.

'Look around,' I said. 'Which idiot do you think was on a Welsh hillside at 5 o'clock this morning in the pouring rain, up to his neck in shit, burying an Eslan?'

* * *

A cautionary tale. The following is the true account of how the Intendant (Chief Executive) of the Deutsches Schauspielhaus Hamburg and joint Artistic Director of the English Shakespeare Company, found himself on his hands and knees in Block G of North Terminal Car Park at Gatwick Airport, his index finger up the exhaust of his car, crying.

Dear Diary.

To Hamburg Airport in the usual panic. London for a meeting in Piccadilly with the Arts Council of Great Britain. Attempt to check in. Yes, I know the name on my passport is Bogdin. Bogdanov is my professional name. Ukrainian. And watch out for independence. I'll have two passports, Ukrainian and Welsh.

Through, perspiring. Glance at the indicator board. No delay. Buy yesterday's *Guardian*. Sit. Squeeze in between what looked like a Bavarian wrestler and a Turkish weight-lifter to read Michael 'Bunter' Billington – hailing, saluting, welcoming, but, on the other hand, unable to help being worried by Ian McKellen.

'Lufthansa regrets to announce the cancellation of all flights to London until further notice'.

What?! Dash to the information desk. The gap between Bavarian and Turk closes as if I had never been. 'Technical

83

problems sir.' One flight only that will get me to London in time for the meeting. Via Gatwick. Hamburg Airlines. The next technological step up from a glider. One hundred people fighting for ten places.

'But I must get to London this afternoon, it's a matter of life and death.'

'Would Mr Bogdanov please come to the Lufthansa desk.'

Smirk, smirk. Priority. Frequent Flyer. There are some compensations.

Two hours delay. Will just make it to the meeting. Oh well. One problem.

My car is at Heathrow, thirty five miles away with a firm called 'Flyaway'. Ring them, see if it's possible for them to drive it to Gatwick.

'Extra cost, sir, call us on arrival and we'll tell you where we've left it.'

Up the stairs of the snub nose aircraft, its little eyes watching us all the way, lugging the largest piece of illegal hand luggage in the world.

God! I've left my small black shoulder bag with my whole life in it in the terminal! Push back down the steps. 'Excuse me! Excuse me! Entschuldigung!' Lug, lug. Run to the bus which has just closed its doors. Face pressed against the moving glass. 'Excuse me, I must get back to the terminal, I've left a bag.'

'Where?'

'Underneath a Tartar.'

'Quick sir'. Fast drive to the terminal. Dash in. The seats are now occupied by an Indian lady and a Prussian officer.

'Excuse me'. Undignified scramble on hands and knees under the seats, lady clutching her sari suspiciously. No, they haven't seen a small black bag. Desperately crawling around. The crowded lounge watching me curiously. Ancient British custom.

'Sorry, sir, the flight will have to go, it's late already.' Understatement. Maybe I've left it at the bookstall. Dash out to the shopping area through passport control. Bag not there.

'Sorry sir, I'm letting the flight go, if we find the bag we can send it on.'

'You don't understand, it's got my life in it.'

'Sorry, sir, the flight must go'. She puts a call through.

I can't get on without my life.

Nightmare scenario: midnight plane to Heathrow. Car now at Gatwick. Trail disconsolately back through security.

Now, what is this, perched smugly on top of the x-ray machine, winking at me with its little brass clasp? You little . . .

'Yours, sir? Can you prove it?' In desperation, emptying everything out all over the conveyor belt, babbling incoherent descriptions in incoherent German. Too much of an idiot to be smuggling drugs and bombs.

'Wait, wait!' Breathlessly informing the Hamburg Airlines lady 'I've got it, by Jove, I've got it!'

'I think the flight's gone sir, but I'll just ring through.'

Calloo, Callay! They're still winding up the elastic band. We thumb a lift with a passing bus. Up the stairs and run the gauntlet of baleful stares from passengers now running three hours late. Sorry, Sorry. Must learn to swim. Takes longer but less nerve racking.

We land on one wheel – angle of forty-five degrees. Dash through to the nearest phone box. 'Your car, sir, is in the car park, level G Row 6. The keys are up the exhaust.'

Set off, the merest hint of a suspicion of a spring in my step. Down the tunnel and across the road. Wait a minute. Where's my bag? Oh no! I must have left it on top of the phone.

Panic, in the pit of.

It's still there, nobody's taken it. Relief. Back down the tunnel. Over the road, into the car park to level G. Into lift. Need to press 'G'. A-B-C-D . . . where's E, F and G? . . . must have forgotten to add them. No – there must be stairs. Get out at D. Attempt to find stairs. There is none. In the gap above D, where E and F should be there is nothing but air, sky, clouds, birds, sunshine and laughter. Ha, Ha. I can't believe it. Nearest phone? Back in the terminal . . .

Lift, road, tunnel, phone.

'Hello, Flyaway? There is no level G.'

'What Terminal are you in?'

'There is only one terminal at Gatwick.'

'They've just opened a new one – North. That's where the car is.'

'Why the f— didn't you say so in the first place?'

Risk a molestation charge as I grab desperately at a backpacker.

'Excuse me, madam, what terminal is this?'

'South.'

Wonderful. The North terminal is a computer, sprinter, South East Network, British Rail is getting you there, train ride away. I get out at the far end and – this is the point at which the story takes on an air of surreal unbelievability, and where you stop reading because the imagination is taking over to such an extent that you are convinced that the writer and victim of this little extravaganza is pulling all four legs at once. But stay with it, it gets worse and it's all true.

Hands up, there, who knows what I've left behind for the third time?

Back into the train, this time stomach really sinking. I know it's not going to be there. I know it's not going to be there. It isn't. Just a man trying to ring Caracas with 20p. Run to the short term attendant.

'A small black bag, John?'

'Yes, yes, that's the one.'

'It's over there, John.'

Turn and look. A circle of six helmeted policemen are standing looking suspiciously at an object sitting on the ground in the middle of them. My bag. Try to attract their attention by circling outside the broad blue backs, jumping up and down and squeaking in a high voice.

'Excuse me, excuse me! That's my bag!'

(SLOWLY) 'Is this your bag, sir?'

(QUICKLY) 'Yes, yes. That's what I've been trying to say. It's my bag.'

(SLOWLY) 'Oh, so it's your bag, is it? We thought it was a bomb.'

They didn't ask me to prove it. Our policemen are wonderful. Tie the bag to my belt. Grimly get back on the train. North Terminal. All change for Kumquat Airlines. Car Park. Level G. Right where it should be. No gap, no hole. Not AWOL. The very epitome of what a late twentieth century concrete car park level, six stories up, should be. And there's the car. Right where it should be. Ahhh. A feeling like Hannibal finally cresting the Alps and seeing a Starbucks . . .

Perspiring, my ample frame now reduced to a mere six and a half stone with all the exertion, I kneel as if in supplication, in prayer, in gentle deference to the cylindrical rear-end god of a Volkswagen Golf, the exhaust pipe. Or, to give it its Teutonic form – the *Auspuff*.

Arse skywards – VW *Auspuffers* are rather low on the ground – I delicately insert my index finger into the carbon coated orifice.

Not delicately enough.

The tip of my finger touches the cold metal of the ignition key and pushes it a crucial centimetre up the pipe. I wildly rotate my finger, coating my whole hand in black oil and soot. The key remains tantalisingly out of reach. I begin to cry. There's more, there's more . . .

The story of how I finally retrieved the key one hour later,

with the help of an AA man, a car park attendant, two shop
assistants, a small dog, a Japanese lady with a pushchair and a bent
wire coat hanger from a shopping centre in Crawley, will have to
wait . . . The point of the story is I missed the meeting. Gave a
performance instead. The comedy of errors.

9

Kept in the Dark

Church halls, pubs, attics, clubs, basements, foyers, front rooms, offices – actors emerge on to stage like moles blinking in the light, crawling, mixed metaphorically, like drowned rats out of some dark infested hole, to strut in ruff and frill, sporting such ostentatious names as Doriment, Celemene, Bassanio, Aguecheek. The chandeliers, the posh seats, the decorative artifice of the costumes and design, might transport an audience into a world of seductive and elusive elegance, but the creative process is like Holden Caulfield's rusty razor.

Very few modern theatres are designed with adequate or practical back stage facilities let alone proper rehearsal spaces and, in older theatres, they are virtually unknown. Like motorway parking areas or refreshment stops, the money runs out at the planning stage and the first things to be cut are the very things that make for the essential smooth and efficient running of a building. I've had it up to here with rehearsals that take place in rooms that are black holes, no natural light, in temperatures that oscillate between sauna and deep freeze, with one broken toilet and fungus on the walls. Were the laws governing conditions in the work-place to be applied to theatre, most shows would never see the light of stage.

Why is it that this most precious and essential of commodities, the large, naturally lit, ventilated rehearsal space, is the last thing that architects consider? I have seen actors break ankles on concrete floors, go through the rotting boards of an upstairs gallery; I have rehearsed musicals in the acoustic equivalent of a Jumbo slipstream, dance routines on surfaces akin to the Quantocks, fights in a phone box, songs in a sink, sonnets to the accompaniment of lute, lyre and the roadworks at Spaghetti Junction. I have rehearsed in the snow in Canada (and the Royal Court Theatre Upstairs), in the wind in Chicago, on the beach in Sierra Leone, in the bus station in Leicester; suffered earthquakes in Japan and the toilets of the Territorial Army Headquarters in Wandsworth (wonderful for choral harmonies). I have been turfed out because of brass bands, council meetings, prayer groups, sewing circles, karate, table tennis, bingo, badminton and Buddhism. Oh yes, and other rehearsals. I have been double-booked, treble-booked, un-booked or not booked at all. In London I have trekked from Hornchurch to Hampton and from Uxbridge to Eltham. The cost in hires, travel, faxes, phones, texts, bikes, vans, person hours – have sometimes been the equivalent of a whole production.

In 1986/7 the ESC technical rehearsal periods for *The Henrys* and *The Wars of the Roses*, were characterised by two of the roughest and toughest spaces and fit-ups it has ever been my misfortune to experience. I wouldn't wish them on a dog, never mind a director and team. (Unfair to dogs, I hear you cry).

We celebrated the end of rehearsals for *The Henrys* in London with some champagne and sandwiches at Awful House (trade name – Alford House, Kennington) and then headed for Plymouth for the final two weeks prior to opening at the Theatre Royal. Our technical fit-up was to take place at the headquarters of RAF Mountbatten, in a gigantic disused hangar on the sea front. (Real helicopters took off and landed during rehearsals of the battle sequences in *Henry V*. It was like preparing for the Falklands). The Theatre Royal had rigged up our set, lights and sound in this vast, cavernous, corrugated and concrete space, where we had to prepare technically and dress rehearse the three shows prior to opening cold, (in all senses) with virtually no time on stage, on a Monday night. In the parlous state of the Arts a theatre cannot afford to lose income being 'dark'.

I rolled into the hangar late on Sunday night to begin our fortnight nightmare. It was cold, it was wet, it was windy. It was November. The sea spray and gales lashed against the corrugated sides of the hangar. The rain torrented, the wind howled, the blow heaters blew, the company performed heroically. Skips and skips of costumes, on loan and eventually hired from the Royal National Theatre, were sifted through, tried on, accepted, rejected, as we attempted to fit the characters, scene and mood. In no time, the props and costumes were filthy as they lay on the floor. John Woodvine for the first time in gigantic white pudding padding, more like Michelin Man than Falstaff. The uniforms didn't gel with the bentwood chairs and the collapsible tables. The sandbags leaked. The sliding screen . . . didn't. The white cloths wouldn't billow, pillow or create snowy landscapes. More a case of the *Hesperus* crossed with a St Moritz thaw. The screens jammed, broke, tore, wouldn't close, warped. Made on the cheap.

The lighting firm White Light twice landed us with a bum lighting board. The tank, collapsible, used for the siege of Harfleur, was a real wobbly old Heath Robinson affair, the framework held together with pins. Michael Pennington leapt on it, staggered, regained his balance and with smoke bellowing around him, obscuring both face and voice began 'Once more unto the breach' . . . the tank fell apart. Four weeks into the tour it disappeared from the production altogether.

And yet somehow fourteen days later we moved in to the theatre to open *Henry IV Part 1* on Monday night with a full rehearsal of each of the plays behind us. Wednesday was *Henry IV Part 2*, Friday *Henry V* and then on Saturday, with no chance of a dry run, the plays unprepared technically, morning, afternoon and evening, all three. It was chaos. Costumes and props were A.W.O.L and no let-up in the afternoon or evening. No breaks for anyone from 8 am until midnight.

Exhausted we stood on the stage that Saturday night, having opened all three in five days, and then presented the trilogy in the space of twelve hours for the first time. As the cheers rang out I thought 'How stupid can we get?' See below for answer.

* * *

November again, this time 1987. Doesn't time fly? We moved into our end phase for *The Wars of the Roses*, our seven-part version of the history cycle from *Richard II* to *Richard III*. Our eventual destination was The Theatre Royal Bath.

We were in what was laughingly called a 'studio' in Limehouse. It was an old storage warehouse, barely large enough, measuring some fifty foot by seventy. One end had a huge entrance, obviously for container lorries, and no doors. It would have to be blocked up. So would the holes in the roof, the holes in the walls. . . . It had been the mildest of autumns but, as luck would have it, the weather turned nasty for the two weeks that we were there. Rain, wind, snow, sleet, we had everything the Thames, ten metres away, could throw at us. We had underestimated and underbudgeted the extras.

Simon Opie, Production Manager, put two Portacabins outside the dock-doors for emergency dressing rooms (the main ones were some several hundred yards away across the compound). They had to be heated. The familiar sound of propane blow-heaters filled the air in the 'studio'. But, whereas in the hangar at Plymouth they were some way away from the action, here we were right on top of them. They could not be kept going during rehearsal.

We froze.

I set up a small electric blow heater under my chair. This I relinquished for long spells to Clyde Pollitt, who was turning purple in the cold. I feared for him. Clyde only had one lung, was a fragile sixty-three, but would never complain. We rehearsed in overcoats, gloves, mufflers . . . at one stage a chunk of the roof blew in. Simon hired a heater that pumped air in through a tube from the outside; it was fiendishly expensive. We had the same scramble on costumes as the year before. One of our Assistant Stage Managers finally walked out, disappeared and could not be found. We replaced him with one week to go.

Mark Henderson had taken over the lighting from Chris Ellis, who was heavily engaged in his home theatre, the Haymarket in Leicester. Unfortunately, Mark was only partly available, working at that time at the Royal National Theatre. His schedule had been tight anyway, and due to our postponing the whole production a week, he would be unavailable in Bath. In Limehouse we were sitting too close to the action. The subtlety of the lighting from that distance was to prove useless when we got onto the big stage. I had to start re-lighting the seven shows from the beginning, a situation that I never properly caught up with.

We froze on. Coughs and colds notwithstanding, we managed to get some sort of a run of all seven plays. There was an awful lot left to do in Bath. The pattern for the opening there was as follows:

Tuesday 8th December: *Richard II*; Wednesday 9th: *Henry IV Part 1*; Thursday 10th: *Henry IV Part 2*; Friday 11th: *Henry V*; Saturday 12th: *Richard II* and *Henry IV Parts 1 and 2*; Monday 14th: *Henry VI House of Lancaster*; Tuesday 15th: *Henry VI House of York*, Wednesday 16th: *Richard III*.

I don't suppose we can claim a world record, but opening twenty four hours of Shakespeare in nine days, is not bad going. Don't boast, don't complain. Why bother? What's the point? What are you trying to prove? A familiar argument ran: 'If the circumstances are so rushed and the compromises so great, what's the point of it all? Why fuck up a great set of plays just to show you can get them on? Anyone can do shoddy, ill-prepared, technically unsound work'.

It was an achievement just to get them on.

But the reasons for doing it ran much deeper. Despite all the obvious drawbacks, there was paradoxically one great advantage. Artistic freedom. Even if the compromises at times seemed unending, in another way the line was straight and true. The release of the language, the quality of the story-telling, at its best, was exhilarating. Nobody can get a production right. As a director, you do one good one, one bad one, one medium. You spend your time trying to eliminate the bad one. Then, with one good and two medium, you're pretty good. With two good and one medium, you're world class. And here we were with seven on offer. It's a very simple equation really. If you get 90% of a production right (what is right?), you are a world beater. At 75% it is a great production and about the most that any self-respecting director can hope for. The problem with getting even 75% of *The Wars of the Roses* right, however, is that while out of twenty-four hours eighteen might be passable, that still leaves six whole hours that are naff! That's two whole plays! ('Which two?' I hear you cry. Opinions vary.)

And if Bath Theatre Royal had been too small the year before, 1986, when we had presented *The Henrys* there on tour, this time it was pretty catastrophic. We knew the routine, however. Open up the scene dock and build a platform out the back in the street for the lights, to store the props, etc.,. The weather in December this year was mercifully mild, no repeat of last year's audience deep freeze, when a howling gale in sub zero conditions had turned the stalls into a Siberian refugee camp.

Technically, none of the shows was up to much and *House of York* and *Lancaster* were very messy. Each of them contained twenty-four fast moving scenes. They needed tightening.

The best was Richard III. It was clear that Andy Jarvis as the

Leicester Car Park King was going to deliver all that he had promised in rehearsal, and the last two scenes were sensational. Andy's armour only just arrived on the afternoon of the opening and, when he donned it, we discovered to our horror that the hump had been built on the wrong side of his back. In a series of frantic phone calls, we ascertained that there was just enough time to get it changed. We had done it on the cheap. Straps and buckles were to break and bits fly off – one of the penalties of tight budgets. The 'quick change' in and out of the costume on that first performance took an eternity.

Why do we do it? Please Anton, Henrik, Bert and Will, don't let me, make me stop. Above all let me not rehearse anymore in London. I can't take any more tube strikes, sprinter failures, Connex incompetence, bomb scares, snow, leaves, donkeys on the line, excuses for lateness. Let me have a small group living communally up in the hills, with good wine and good food and a hundred foot square centrally heated, Velux windowed barn to rehearse in and where the only problem is who's sleeping with whom.

(The rehearsal period of the Henrys and The Wars of the Roses reprinted from 'The English Shakespeare Company – The Story of The Wars of the Roses'.)

10

We'll let you know

I hate auditions, it's an humiliating process. The clichés about them are all true. 'Thank you, next please.' 'Don't ring us, we'll ring you.' 'We'll know by tomorrow.' 'Have you got anything else?' 'Marvellous, marvellous! Thank you so much!'

How do you judge an actor's talent on the basis of what is sometimes a demeaning, degrading, humiliating one minute chat and (if you're lucky) two short audition pieces? We directors all know this and yet we all subscribe to it. When casting a production of Mary O'Malley's *Once a Catholic* for the Sheffield Crucible Theatre, the girls all seemed to me to be so gifted that, in a shameful gesture of defiance and protest at the whole ghastly system, I finally opted, with a pin, for a blonde, a brunette and a redhead as the principal requirements of the leading three roles. As basic as that.

I used to opt for an extended workout, putting groups of six or eight together, stretching their versatility over a period of a couple of hours (better still, working with fifty-odd people over a week, mixing the groups up). I used concentration exercises, story telling, invention, improvisation, putting individuals into situations of group inter-dependency, making them accept collective responsibility. Seeing who would opt in, who would opt out. Playing with sounds, language, rhythm, music. Appointing leaders. Finding out their physical limitations, their vocal.

We'll let you know

This is, of course, a luxury. How do you cope with two thousand hopefuls for a musical? Well, singing and dancing are ends in themselves and are somewhat easier to judge by applying certain criteria, but the same cattle market routine still applies. The complicated psychological personality of the actor is somewhat more difficult to assess. The initial star often fades when the going gets rough. The shy, backward introvert turns out to have an inner strength, which reveals itself under pressure. We pride ourselves that as we get older, with the experience of over two hundred and fifty productions behind us, we are able to tell at a glance (well, at a Shakespeare and a Modern) who is able to act well and who not. This is partly true, but usually it means that we're getting lazy. There is no substitute for treating the person hoping to be employed by you with dignity and respect and according that person the courtesy of a thorough investigation of their ability. A luxury for many directors, but most small groups have to work in this way. They cannot afford to make mistakes. ('Neither can we', squeal the commercial producers, clutching their hands to their hearts, but in reality checking that the wallet is still safe inside the breast pocket.)

These days, starting from the basic assumption that someone can act (otherwise they wouldn't be coming to see me), I try and assess an actor's ability through talking – about anything and everything. Learn where they're at, where they're coming from, what points of view we have in common, using a chance remark as a spring-board or working off a c.v. This way I am able to put groups of people together with whom I know I'll enjoy working. I make mistakes – sure – but we make just as many mistakes following any other route. This system is at least humane and I get to meet a lot of interesting people, even if I never get to work with them . . .

Take ten people off the street and seven will be able to act in the conventional sense. Or six. Or all ten. I don't know. The degree of proficiency with which they can perform depends on training, accessibility, opportunity. And once again, within the profession itself, there are actors who succeed, not because of talent but because they have had more opportunity: one is in the right place at the right time, one strikes it lucky in a particular role – on stage, on television. What else can one say about an occupation where at any one time about 80% are unemployed? They can't all be talentless. And as Chekov said over a hundred years ago – 'Nowadays there are few outstandingly gifted actors, but the average actor has improved enormously'. There are very few geniuses and those who leave the profession bitter, disappointed, frustrated, often do so with a justified belief that the gods just didn't deal them the right hand when they dished out the Equity cards.

For some actors, their face didn't fit, they were too 'bolshie', too 'difficult', 'too many hang-ups', 'asked too many questions', 'were too political'. But why should actors be forced to conform to the whoring reputation of the profession merely to get a job? Unfortunately the battle lines are drawn up fairly strictly, between integrity on the one side and the need to survive on the other, combining a fox-like cunning, Heep-like humility and a cynical ability to swear black is white if it means getting a few lines in a soap. 'A good actor must never be in love with anybody but himself'. (Hazlitt).

Children at play – which one will end up the actor? What happens to this imaginative invention as we grow older? Is not acting the mere extension? An attempt to capture the lost world of childhood fantasy? There are those who choose it as a profession and those who perforce, often through circumstance, opt for more grown up things. Like making money . . .

What skills do actors possess that mark them out above others? All start with the same tools – the voice, the body. Both need nurturing, extending, challenging. There is no such thing as the perfect actor, each works within a given range. This sometimes takes the form of an extended personality – many film actors for example – and often leads to the accusation that an actor is merely playing him or herself. This could be a compliment. It is perhaps the hardest thing of all to give all of oneself over to a performance of oneself that is not oneself but someone else. 'And nothing is but what is not' (*Hamlet*).

Then there are others who extend their range both physically and vocally, getting outside of themselves and transforming themselves into something they palpably are not, something alien. Olivier – get the walk right and you'll get the character. (There is something in that, but I guess Stanislavski wouldn't approve).

Acrobatic, musical, vocal skills – the complete actor possesses all these things. And yet possessing them is no guarantee of a great actor. That final element of fantasy, the ability not to be emotional but to express emotion, to make an audience empathise, it is that quality that transcends all other skills. But when you get them all together . . .

Sometimes I'd give anything to have just one of them. How often does a young actor arrive for an audition and say, I learned the piano, the flute, the trumpet to Grade 8, but I gave it up after I left school. Do you work out? I play football. Can you sing? In a chorus. Do you smoke? Only in the evening. How many? About a pack.

Part of the problem is that drama schools have little time to structure a real routine of discipline and training for after the pupil leaves. Courses are often aimed at TV and film careers and the acting is of the 28 inch wide screen square variety or of the whispering, pocket-handkerchief-pub-upstairs kind. Older directors (me) complain that there are fewer young actors than of yore capable of commanding a big stage in a major role and the cases of strained larynx amount almost to an epidemic.

The problem for an actor is that if not acting, they are not an actor. Six months out of work and it can take six months to get back to par. A year out, two years out . . . and so on. Some never get back, particularly those who sell their soul to films, try a comeback on stage and can't make it. Richard Burton, Peter O'Toole, Anthony Hopkins, Nicol Williamson, Richard Harris – the British stage – or rather the Celtic, looking at the above – nearly lost a whole generation of great stage actors through their prolonged absence in film.

The point I'm making is that there is no substitute for physical and vocal discipline, a daily routine, so that, even if out of work for any length of time, steps have been taken to minimise the damage of this enforced layoff – a 'rest'. And my heart weeps with rage for the endless number of drama students who sometimes work a twenty hour day in an attempt to pay their way through college. No discretionary grants, you see.

I like dangerous acting and dangerous actors, (who doesn't) – those who are unpredictable and can stand a scene on its head by doing the unexpected. When such performers are at work, there is an electricity in the air and others are either dragged along in the slip stream or are pushed to dig deep into themselves to find new reserves of creativity.

I do not mean the actor who is wilful, the one who destroys the rhythm of a performance by a gratuitous improvisation that has nothing whatsoever to do with the role or the play. Nor do I mean the selfish actor who ignores the needs of the other performers while being intent on doing their own thing. I mean the actor who looks you in the eye and says 'Come with me on this journey. We're going to break a few sound barriers'. This is not merely a question of 'invention'. The 'inventive' actor is usually just a bundle of tricks that distorts the performance. True invention is organic not trickery. Nor is it a question of misplaced energy. It is just as easy to destroy a performance by over-energising, being frenetic, as it is to under-energise. Pace is not speed. It is a combination of rhythm and energy. No, the actor for me is the one who balances the performance on a knife-edge – will she or he succeed in staying on that edge, or slip and slice the performance in two.

If I have a fault (he said), it is that I do not praise enough. I forget that people are not machines, that they need encouragement, or at least a word to indicate that they are on the right track. Some actors need no more than that, others need a constant reminder that their efforts are not in vain. I tend to leave actors alone if their performance is headed in the right direction and concentrate my attention on those who need help. In other words, 'if I don't say anything, then you're doing all right'. This causes an actor to feel neglected. I know this and am constantly trying to rectify this fault. An actor who is turning in a marvellous performance will come to me and want some criticism. I pick on small things, detail, in order to give something to bite on. What concerns me more is the centre of the performance, the broad sweep, the danger, the bigness. Detail can come later. I like to give actors freedom to express themselves. This often means a lot of thrashing around, for many actors do not know how to use this freedom in a positive way, being still locked into the text-in-the-hand literary, cerebral analysis school of acting and directing. I like to go through a lot of analysis and theory at the beginning of rehearsal and then encourage the actor to abandon the script and let the body take over for a bit from the brain. I encourage them to think politically and act instinctively.

Leaving them alone in the belief that they are coping well has consequences. An actor who appears to be totally calm, working methodically and clearly towards an agreed end, is sometimes nursing a volcanic hysteria masked by a veneer of composure. I encountered one such problem on *Uncle Vanya* at the Royal National Theatre in 1985.

Dinsdale Landen was struggling with Astrov. It was his first straight role in a long time, having had a run of successful comic parts. I was concentrating on his performance and having a difficult time. Cheri Lunghi, Yelena, who had appeared to be completely in command, rehearsing with a sharp, analytical intelligence, carefully building her performance, suddenly flipped. I received a phone call one Sunday, saying that the whole production was a disaster and that I didn't have the intellectual and psychological equipment to deal with the play. I was too conventional. She was asking Peter Hall to take over.

Which she did.

Peter asked me what it was all about. I said 'A clash of method and temperament'. It is true, I had been ignoring her in the belief that Cheri, an experienced and fine actress, was in control of her performance. My problems were other. In the event, poor Dinsdale had a nightmare press night, inaudible, fluffing lines and totally lacking in confidence. A pity. The production was, on balance, a good one, though Cheri, frustrated by my methods, knew that I wasn't pushing her. Those who saw *Uncle Vanya* at the beginning would not have recognised it a dozen or so perform-ances later, when Dinsdale gained confidence. It started to pack the Olivier and I ended up getting an Olivier Nomination for Best Director. You wouldn't have known that, though, from the first night. Cheri never really recovered from the set-back and I blame myself for not seeing the signs and for employing the 'if-it-works-don't-mend-it' method at the wrong time.

Often, in direct contrast to choosing through audition, a lead actor is cast for you by the host theatre – inevitable when working abroad of course – sometimes not even having seen that actor perform. Nevertheless I have made many lasting lifelong friend-ships though the relationship first established on the rehearsal room floor although I can't pretend this is always successful and there are other relationships forged in this way that have ended in mutual alienation. These days I try and work as far as possible with a group with whom I am already familiar – trying to recreate the feeling of the old time rep ensemble. Better the devil you know. One thing I don't do is audition.

11

First Nights

I never watch First Nights. Never.

Directors approach these often hyper-hysterical occasions in differing ways. Some sit in the middle of the stalls, braving all the mistakes and shortcomings of a tense and nervous performance. Others (if the theatre has one), sit in a box, or (if the theatre has one), the director's box, or (if the theatre has one), the lighting/sound booth, where, with the show relay or tannoy turned up full blast, the glass window usually separates the director and assistant/ designer/fight director/choreographer/publicist – whoever happens to gather there in a show of solidarity – from the audience and the worst expletive excesses. Cries of 'Oh no, how could he!' and 'Jesus, the lift has stuck!' and 'Where's the sound, he's missed the sound cue, no not that one you idiot, it's the wrong one!' as thunder rolls out instead of the dulcet sound of a mandolin. This, accompanied by much tearing of hair, drinking of whisky/wine/ vodka and beating of fists, feet, body, head against the wall, chair, floor, door.

The audience is, of course, oblivious to all this, merely believing that the man marooned eight feet up in the air through-out the whole of an intimate love scene is a perverse directorial quirk on the part of insouciant Bogdanov. That the actor bellowing his way through the reflective soliloquies, as if clearing a passage through the fog-bound Dardenelles, has been asked to perform it in that manner. 'And what an interesting thing to hear an owl on the beach. That's what marks a director out'. Not so the critics. 'The whole shoddy, technically deficient, melodramatic evening is one I would prefer to forget. Bogdanov couldn't direct his way out of a *sac de papier*'.

The first night of A Christmas Carol at The Swansea Grand Theatre in 2006 was marked by Ron Moody, Scrooge, having such trouble with his lines that he dried close on eighty times. So unsure was poor old Ron that Erica Eirion, the Assistant Director, took over the prompt book from the Deputy Stage Manager and actually sat on stage to prompt him. 'She's good isn't she?' said Ron to the audience, 'I'll have to get rid of her, she knows it better than I do'. At one point he sat down on the loud-speaker under the balcony and said to the audience – 'This is terrible isn't it?'

'Yes' chorused the audience as they left in their droves. Word reached me in the bar and I went into the performance to share in the rest of the cast's mortification.

Etc., etc., etc.,.

No, I prefer not to put myself through that torture. I remain calm, angelic even, never losing my temper, right up to the last moment. This helps for a smooth technical period and, when others are under pressure and tempers are short, I find it totally unproductive to give way to fits of pique, anger and petulance, flexing the ego muscles, shouting, bawling people out, blaming mistakes on others, calling into question reputations, origins of birth, skills, up-bringing, ability to read, count, see, hear.

Totally unproductive.

It is a lesson I learned early on and it has helped me through many a difficult technical rehearsal where I need all the wit and concentration going to combat the problems as they hurtle towards me. Never panic, merely work methodically to achieve the maximum possible within the given time. Shelve the problems that prove difficult till a later time and, at a certain moment, abandon those that are insoluble. Then, at a point when the dogs of Wardle are let loose, rather than suffer a nervous breakdown because you can no longer do anything about anything and have no desire to witness the wholesale disaster that sometimes occurs on these occasions, you disappear around the corner for a pint, play bar billiards, watch television, go and have a meal, discuss the next project with the designer. Or, as happened on one occasion, the first night of *Hair* at the Old Vic – a perfect example of the above – go and watch another first night, in that instance a show by my son Malachi's group, Torsion Theatre, at the Turtle Key Arts Centre, Fulham. Or settle down in an office with a few chums and a couple of bottles of good wine. Then you stand a fair chance of being pissed at the end of the performance, can go backstage and genuinely congratulate everybody, not on the performance of that evening but on the whole creative period.

That way it doesn't matter if a particular actor has let themselves down that night. You don't have to lie (nobody wants at that moment to hear 'Jesus, you were awful. What on earth did you think you were doing up there?'). You can thank people and pass out bouquets for the whole rehearsal and, if there is one, preview period. When people ask 'How do you think it went?' Reply 'I don't know, I didn't see it.' And watch their faces.

I used to build into a productions a 'guest spot' on First Nights, where anybody who wants to may appear on stage in a party scene, a crowd, a pub – whatever. The entrance of the Players in *Hamlet* is always a good one. Phil Bowen played Hamlet for me at The Old Vic transfer of my Young Vic production in 1989. I used to sit in the Windmill pub next door on first nights in those days and the actors would come dashing in from time to time with reports on how the show was going. Phil Bowen had inveigled an old comedian, Tommy Godfrey, who used to drink in The Windmill, to come on stage with the Players. Sure enough Tommy turned up, half-cut from The Cut, was brought on stage, made a beeline for Phil, shook him by the hand and said "Allo 'Am, 'ow you doin'?'

Although not watching, I used to try on first nights wherever possible to contrive an appearance in these guest spots to show solidarity. (The appearance is better early on before the wine takes over.)

Naturally, there are those plays that do not lend themselves to this Hitchcockian quirk, but I did once suggest to a management that the audience participation element in *The Cherry Orchard* should be a tree chopping competition in the foyer. Nobody took me seriously. Unforunately, try as I will, I am afflicted by insouciance though finally mellowing with age.

An early, dominant memory and example is of, at the age of twelve, singing one extra 'Hallelulja' in the Hallelulja Chorus on Speech Day in the Harrow School Speech Hall to win a sixpenny bet. At the end of the Hallelujas thundering out came this one squeaky voice piping 'Halellulja'. The Choir erupted, one thousand dignitaries and parents sniggered. The Choral master, One-eyed Wilson sacked me. I miscounted, I lied. But I won sixpence.

My avoidance of first nights began as early as 1966. It was a production of *Under Milk Wood* – the first of eleven and one that I would call a benchmark production – at the Players Theatre, Trinity College, Dublin, a production which then later transferred to the Gate Theatre. I had a remarkable cast of eight actors from Players that included Gillian Hannah, Dinah Stabb, Martin Lewis – the newscaster, a good actor – and Shane Bryant, Hammer hero. There were sixty lighting cues in the first ten minutes. Players Theatre had limited facilities, a mixture of about twenty lamps, mostly five hundred watt. The cues were mainly single spot cues, lighting up individual actors in individual areas. On Cue No. 2 the Board operator got one cue behind in the sequence and remained so for the duration. It was rather like a demonstration of German expressionist lighting design. Anywhere the actors were, the lights weren't. A nightmare. It was amazing that the performance recovered from what must have been a most surreal experience. That it did so I wasn't around to witness. I had fled.

As did Bill Dudley, the designer of *Hamlet* on the first night of my opening production as Intendant at the Deutsches Schauspielhaus, Hamburg in 1989. The set was a Bill Dudley special. Three hydraulic rotating and tracking walls and a German special Panzer bridge of seven tons of cast iron that went up and down. They assured me that the guy who had done *Starlight Express* in Bochum was a genius with hydraulics. So much of a genius that, after being on the set for two weeks with nothing working, unable to get a run-through and the first night fast approaching, I called in Mike Barnet from London, the original *Starlight* specialist, who really *is* a genius. Mike managed to solve some of the problems but it was touch and go as to which of the walls would stick first.

The first night arrived. The last complete run-though was a distant two week away memory in the rehearsal room. We held an emergency meeting.

Should we postpone the first night? It was already late in the season for an opening production – the end of October – and the hysteria in the press had reached fever pitch. The whole of the German media mafia were flying in from all points Deutsch to see this Brit fall on his arse. We decided to go ahead and risk disaster. So, what was possibly the most important production of my life of possibly the world's greatest play in Germany's largest National Theatre, opened without a single a run-through.

Everything was fine up to what was staged as the Claudius address-to-the-nation balcony scene. The wall down front of the stage was supposed to revolve from mass concrete to reveal the palace interior on the other side. It wouldn't. Panic. We had about ten minutes to the next change when if it still wouldn't move we were screwed. I would have to go on stage and apologise and abandon the production.

Unthinkable.

I was in the wings, crying, and the company were standing at the back of the stage wondering what to do. I ran onto stage, hidden by the wall, and gestured that they should try and carry on. The cast entered from the same door, through which they had exited, to play the sumptuous interior palace scene in front of a concrete bunker.

I ran underneath the stage to where the hydraulic controls were situated. There were Gerd Schlesselmann (my deputy), Mike Barnett and Lothar, the Buehnenmeister (Master Carpenter), wrestling with spanners and monkey wrenches, sweating and trying to turn a huge nut that was leaking oil all over them. I couldn't watch. Feeling sick I ran upstairs to stand in the wings, fear wrenching my gut as the moment approached when I would have to step out and stop the show. Bill Dudley ran from the auditorium, out of the theatre, across the road, through the Central Station, down the Monkerbergstrasse and didn't stop running until he reached the Town Hall some half a mile away.

The scene ended. 'It is not nor it cannot come to good' said Uli Tukur, Hamlet (in German of course) and left the stage.

I took a pace forward.

Suddenly there was a 'ping' and the wall shuddered into life and tracked back. And for the rest of the show everything worked like a dream.

Someone up there (or down) liked me after all.

Schlesselmann joined me in the wings, oil from head to foot. We hugged each other. We got a run-through after all – our very first – that first night. It lasted an interminable four and a half hours. Once the show was up and running it came in three-quarters of an hour shorter. The Germans, used to the arse-paralysing length and slowness of a Peter Stein or Juergen Gosch production, didn't see anything wrong. A bit long said one or two of the critics. Too fucking right. And you should be so lucky.

* * *

Which brings me to the first night of *The Seagull* at the Nissai Theatre, for the Toho Theatre Company in Tokyo in 1983.

Kiyoshi Furukawa, one of Toho's leading producers, came to me and said –

'Micar San, on first night you sit next to British Ambassador.'

I said, 'No, I'm sorry, I never watch first nights.'

'No, no, you sit next to British Ambassador.'

'Look, I really am terribly sorry and it may be difficult to understand, but I really never do watch first nights. Arigato. Thank you.'

'No, no, Micar San, you sit next to British Ambassador.'

'Look, let me explain. The problem is. . . .'

Then I thought, this is being a bit churlish. Here I am, a foreigner, a guest in this country, being asked as a courtesy to sit next to the Ambassador . . .

I gave in. 'Okay, just this once, I'll make an exception.'

Now *The Seagull* begins with the construction of a little wooden stage in the grounds of Arkadina's house for the performance of her son Trepliev's play. Chris Dyer the designer and I decided that we would like to begin by building the real stage first as the audience were entering the auditorium, finishing with the artificial one and, from the wholesale chaos and cacophony of a building construction site, home in on the sound of a single hammer knocking in the last nail. In theatre, what is illusory and what is real? How far can you take illusion before it appears to be reality? This is something that constantly occupies me (see *The Taming of the Shrew*, *The Canterbury Tales*, *The Knight of the Burning Pestle*, *The Venetian Twins*).

In Tokyo, theatre begins more often than not at six o'clock, sometimes earlier, the audience coming straight from their place of work and arriving at the last minute. There is also a kamikaze production approach to first nights – it's a do or die affair after one single dress rehearsal. On this occasion, I sent the Toho Construction Team, thirty overalled, yellow hatted technicians out onto stage at twenty minutes to six, 5.40 p.m., and the building started. Cranes hauled massive girders into place, planks were hammered down, lighting bars swung aloft, the sound and sight of drills, arc lights, welders filled the stage. At 6.05 the quiet tapping into place of the last nail on the simple little stage was all that could be heard. Perfect. Twenty-five minutes start to finish.

Come the next day, the first night, I figured that, with the adrenalin flowing, the team would speed up, having already had a chance to practice the set-construction once, and I gave instructions for them to go out five minutes later than the dress rehearsal, at 5.45. Even if things didn't speed up that much, with one thousand five hundred people to seat in the theatre, it was better for the show to start a bit later. And I went off to the reception for the British Ambassador.

I had reckoned without Japanese efficiency.

The technical director, wanting to be doubly sure that we started on time, countermanded my instructions and, instead of sending the crew out five minutes later at 5.45, he sent them out five minutes earlier at 5.35.

They speeded up.

I accompanied the British Ambassador into the auditorium at 5.55 and, to my horror, saw that the false stage was nearly complete. Then, in front of my eyes (I can see it now!), as I stood paralysed, incapable of doing anything about the Shinkansen bullet-train hurtling towards me, the stage manager came out (he can't! He can't!) gave a pre-arranged signal to the lighting box, the house lights went out, the stage dimmed, out came Masha and Medvedenko and two of the most famous lines in Western drama 'Why do you always wear black?' 'Because I'm in mourning for my life' were uttered to the sound of one thousand five hundred people stumbling into the auditorium in the dark, the words totally inaudible over the noise of seats lifting up and down and people falling over each other apologising profusely. I made my excuses to the British Ambassador and, like Bill Dudley, fled. To the nearest bar. I never went back. I never saw the British Ambassador again. I don't know what he thought. I never watch first nights.

The Dubliners

Michael Bogdanov
age 19 return from Paris
1959

Cast *Os Dos Cabelleros
Di Verona*,
Sao Paulo

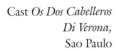

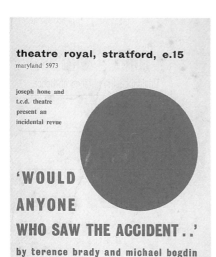

theatre royal, stratford, e.15
maryland 5973

joseph hone and
t.c.d. theatre
present an
incidental revue

'WOULD
ANYONE
WHO SAW THE ACCIDENT . .'

by terence brady and michael bogdin

AND 'THE DUMB WAITER' BY HAROLD PINTER

Left:
Theatre Royal
Stratford East Revue,
the subject of Milton Schulman's
other kind of review!

Below:
A Midsummer Night's Dream
Sketch of Sally Jacob's Set, RSC

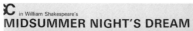

in William Shakespeare's
MIDSUMMER NIGHT'S DREAM

Directed by Peter Brook
Designed by Sally Jacobs
Music by Richard Peaslee, the musicians, the actors, and Felix Mendel

Michael Bryant and
Dan Massey
The Mayor of Zalamea
NT

Bill Wallis as Feste
Twelfth Night
The Wales Theatre Company

Jonathan Pryce and
David Suchet
The Taming of The Shrew
RSC

Macbeth poster of Witches banned by the London Underground

The Witches *Macbeth* ESC

Michael Pennington *Macbeth* ESC

Michael Bogdanov at *The Henrys* readthrough ESC

John Pryce as Pistol *The Wars of the Roses Henry IV Part 2* ESC 1986–1989

Michael Bogdanov and Michael Pennington *The Wars of the Roses The Henrys*' readthrough

Andrew Jarvis *Richard III The Wars of the Roses* ESC

The Company *The Wars of the Roses* the last night in Swansea, final call

Poster and scene from
The Romans in Britain

Michael Bogdanov outside the
Old Bailey

Howard Brenton

Michael Bogdanov
outside Deutsches Schauspielhaus,
Hamburg as Intendant 1989

Uli Wildgruber as Prospero
The Tempest in Hamburg 1991

Michael Bogdanov and Gottfried Greifenhagen
Dramaturg discussing *Maria Stewart*

Michael Bogdanov at a readthrough of *Hamlet*

Der Bundespräsident und Freifrau von Weizsäcker

bitten

zu Ehren Ihrer Majestät Elizabeth II

Königin des Vereinigten Königreichs Großbritannien und Nordirland

und Seiner Königlichen Hoheit Prinz Philip Herzog von Edinburgh

Herrn Intendanten Michael Bogdanov und Frau Bogdanov

zu einem Abendessen im Schloß Augustusburg, Brühl,

am Montag, dem 19. Oktober 1992, um 20.00 Uhr.

Antwort auf beiliegender Karte
erbeten bis 9. Oktober 1992
Tel. (02 28) 17 24 09
Fax (02 28) 17 33 85

Es wird gebeten, die Anfahrt bis 19.45 Uhr zu beenden.
Diese Einladung gilt zugleich als Einlaßkarte.

Frack / Orden
Smoking
Uniform / Orden
Abendkleid

Invitation to a banquet with HRM (on a State visit to Germany in 1992)
at the Augustusburg Palace in Bruehl

Above:
Gerd Garbers in *The Dresser*,
Kammerspiele, Hamburg

Middle:
Johannes Silberschneider
and Timo Dierkes in
Waiting for Godot,
Kammerspiele, Hamburg

Right:
Uli Tukur *Hamlet*
Schauspielhaus, Hamburg

Boris Aljinovic and Peter Theiss in *Elling*, Kammerspiele, Hamburg

Komaki as Nina and Toshi
as Trigorin in *The Seagull*

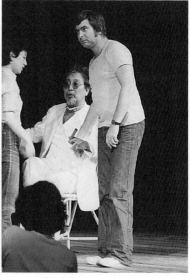

Michael Bogdanov and Sam
(translator) and Hitoshi Tagaki
as Sorin in *The Seagull*.

Michael Bogdanov and Chris Dyer, set designer and
cast round model of the set, *The Seagull*.

芸術座7・8月特別公演

かもめ

アントン・チェーホフ=作
倉橋健=訳
マイケル・ボグダノフ=演出
クリス・ダイヤー=美術

気紛れな恋の風が
湖を吹きぬける時…
翼を傷めた若者が
哀しい愛に旅立った

製作=古川清
織田潤

7月4日初日⇒8月29日
好評前売中/8月分は
7月5日発売中

東宝
ヒビヤ
芸術座

Leaflet for *The Seagull*, Tokyo

Romeo and Juliet RSC and Tokyo production

Ron Moody as Scrooge
Wales Theatre Company

Andrew Jarvis as Richard III, the armour that had the hump
on the wrong side

John Woodvine and Julie Saunders as Prospero and Miranda in *The Tempest*
ESC wearing the plimsoles of the Coveney Criticism

John Dougall as Prince Hal
The Nicholas De Jong review 1988

Michael Bogdanov in the auditorium of the Swansea Grand Theatre

12

Japan

My first visit to Japan was in 1972 with Brook's *Dream* but *The Seagull* was my first of four productions in Tokyo, plus visits from the ESC including opening the Tokyo Globe Theatre with *The Wars of the Roses*.

Japanese actors are dynamite; fearless and a powerhouse of emotion once they let the inscrutable mask slip. In Japan the director is God (or Buddha). I once attended a rehearsal of *The Cherry Orchard* in Tokyo and was appalled to witness the actor playing Yasha go down on his knees, beg forgiveness for some fault and kiss the feet of the director, who screamed and hit him before finally banishing the actor from the theatre, apparently not to return until he had learned true humility. His crime? Questioning whether a move he had been asked to perform was necessary.

And fearless? I was sitting in the front row of a pocket-handkerchief theatre, The Jean Jean Arts Centre, seating fifty, on the ninth floor of a tower block in the Shinjaku district, watching a performance of *King John*, directed by Norio Deguchi, who in the space of five years had worked his way through the entire Shakespeare canon, when suddenly about thirty actors erupted onto the hanky and proceeded to beat the shit out of each other in a whirlwind of arms, legs and batons. I desperately tried to scramble over the back of the seats as a body landed on top of me, having a close encounter of the intimate kind in the process with a lady sitting behind me.

113

In Tokyo the actors work long hours without breaks. However, they do not like starting too early – understandable in a city where it can take two hours to get home and which is one of the world's great all-nighters. Sometimes in Roppongi, a club and theatre district, the traffic at 4.00 a.m. is reminiscent of rush hour at Junction 4 of the M25. Invariably, though, at whatever time rehearsal begins the actors are there beforehand, changed, warmed up and ready to start work on the dot. Disconcertingly, the stage manager blows a whistle and all leap to their feet. Two days of that and you gently remove the whistle never to return it. (I confess to using a whistle myself for German crowd scenes – sometimes necessary when fifty *statisten* – extras – start arguing all at the same time.)

But this discipline and degree of concentration on the part of the Japanese performer is a great bonus. The work is thorough and productive. There can be, however, a problem with improvisation and any experiment involving individual choice. The tendency is to follow the leader. I looked on in amazement during rehearsals for *Romeo and Juliet* at the Imperial Theatre in 1996 as thirty actors, in the course of an improvisation, all circled clockwise limping on their left leg. On explaining that I was after an individual walk from each one of them (very complicated exercise this, deeply psychological), they all turned round and limped anti-clockwise on the right leg. However, perhaps as a result of the way that they are treated by their directors, Japanese actors respond marvellously to a little democratic involvement. Shy at first, they then embrace discussion enthusiastically and the freedom to try things out. 'But of course, Michar San, we do what you want'.

Japanese texts go right to left and up and down. In the middle of one page of THE SEAGULL in capital letters was the word ROTTO. It's a game I was told. I had a vision of some wonderful card-version of cads behaviour, before realising that the Japanese inability to pronounce 'L's had resulted in an 'R' in print. The game was Lotto.

My first encounter with this linguistic foible was at the check-in desk on my first trip to Japan where the air hostess said, with a charming smile, 'Enjoy your fright'. I would then collect these gems in song form – 'All you need is rub', 'She rubs you, yeah, yeah, yeah', 'Wouldn't it be rubbery – rubbery – rubbery'. By and large, apart from occasioning the odd laugh, it brought about very little confusion on the rehearsal floor, until my visit to the Globe (Grobe) Theatre, Tokyo in 1994. There was a 'run-off' on one side of the stage that needed moving. I asked the technician, 'Would you mind moving that ramp up stage, please? He looked baffled. 'Which ramp?' 'That one there.' He wandered off. Half an hour later, I asked him, 'Is there a problem with the ramp?' 'Oh no, I've moved it.' He pointed to a projector on the side of the proscenium which was now in a totally wrong position. I pointed at the run-off 'No, no, not Lamp, Ramp! – Rook, I mean look.' 'Oh, you mean Lamp not Ramp! Okay, Michar-San, reave it to me.'

What are the advantages/disadvantages of working in translation? Mostly the work is not so much an accurate transposition from one language to another as an interpretation. This transition brings about a great freedom, even when (or especially when) the translator is a proven playwright. However, the plays become more about ideas, the language often sacrificed and one is at the mercy of an interpretation at one stage removed, someone else's view. Working in translation can never be anything other than an approximation, and often the better route is an unashamed adaptation into the vernacular, culture and customs of a country. Accept the difficulties, embrace the difference, relish the freedom. The first thing to master directing in any language that you do not speak – is the different speech rhythms. It takes half as long again to say something in Japanese as it does in English. With a

Shakespeare text this means that you are usually half a line ahead, unable to make head or tail of the action with which the actor is accompanying the words. A case of mentally climaxing too soon. It's a question of listening to and absorbing the speech patterns and mentally slowing down as you follow the English text. Eventually you chain this rhythm and are able to make sense of what the actor is saying. It is interpretation by instinct, listening to the actor's voice, watching the body language, trying to separate out the false from the true. This last is identifiable in any culture and any language. Bad acting is bad acting anywhere – emotional excess, melodrama, inaudibility, histrionics, uncontrolled vocal tricks, physical inability – these are common coinage.

The big problem with transferring from one cultural base to another is that, irrespective of the fact that the performance you are schooling the actors in is inevitably an imitation of an English one, the actors are working in their native tongue. The only way one has of interpreting a text – the emotions, the politics, the relationships etc., is through one's own culture. Inevitably, it is an attempt to impose, however unintentional, one's own rhythm on the performance even though, because of the language barrier, there can never be anything more than an approximation of that rhythm. And when you have achieved a production of *The Seagull* that you think would pass muster, there is no way of knowing whether the Japanese audiences will laugh it off the stage or not. Here you are at the mercy of your actors and interpreters to advise you on what, to a Japanese ear, is (a) a good and (b) a strange inflection, there being usually no such thing as a dramaturg or literary adviser to fall back on. You are totally dependent on your translation and have no way of knowing how successful it is except through what your actors tell you and, even then, they are often at variance with each other. It is, therefore, essential to ensure that, if there is to be a new translation of any English play, that it is done in conjunction with a native English speaker. This (a) ensures that the rhythm of the language is properly captured and (b) that the peculiarities of the English language, subtext, pun, buried cultural references, etc., are not misunderstood and misinterpreted. Modern English plays are a minefield in this respect. I have spent many a puzzling and frustrated time unable to comprehend why an actor was failing to do something that was basic and simple according to the English text, finally to realise that the original and the translation were totally at variance with each other.

In the early days in particular (what are we talking about here – 1980), it was difficult to find anyone who spoke English at all and foreigners were thin on the ground. Most of the time communication was through a translator (or translators). This produces a discipline of thought and expression – the need to articulate ideas with economy, clarity and the minimum of circumlocution. I had never realised, until I went through this experience while directing *The Seagull* what a mental strain this concentration exerts and how dependent I had been in Britain on shorthand expletives to explain my meaning. 'She just wants a fuck' speaks volumes about motive. . . .

After a month of holding myself in during rehearsals, only speaking English through the auspices of my translators, two wonderful sisters Tina and Sam Aoke, who although born in Australia, were somewhat grammatically challenged in English, I was invited to lunch in a restaurant by the head of the British Council. We sat opposite each other, he in a suit and tie using a knife and fork, me in jeans and sweatshirt wielding chopsticks, and suddenly the pent-up linguistic frustration of the last month burst from me as the flood-gates opened. Expletives poured forth as S-word followed C-word followed F-word followed B-word, each one accompanied by an abject apology and a stammering explanation.

'Oh shit, I said fuck. Oh fuck, I said cunt. Oh bugger, I said bollocks. Oh fuck it, I'm terribly sorry'.

He sat there daintily crossing knife over fork completely unperturbed.

'That's quite alright, old boy'.

The Seagull brought me face to face with the question to which the trial of *The Romans in Britain* would partially give rise – the difference between an act that is simulated and an act that is illusion – (or can it be both at the same time?). The actress playing Nina, Komaki Kurihara, later to be seen at the Edinburgh Festival and the Royal National Theatre in Ninagawa's production of *Macbeth*, would not kiss Trigorin (Toshi Hosakawa).

She had two techniques, both of which created the illusion of a kiss.

One – Komaki would take Toshi's head between her hands, bring it to her face and, at the last moment, insert her thumbs as a gate between his lips and hers, thereby planting a passionate kiss on her own thumbs. (What is it about thumbs?)

Two – she would enfold him in her arms, traditional style, swing his head downstage so that her own head was masked and gnaw away at his cheek, once again not touching his lips. Both gave the illusion of a kiss. I asked her to kiss him openly, explaining that I was after simulation, not illusion. In this instance, the kiss would have been real, the audience would have witnessed it taking place but, the motive would have been pretence. (Actors might dislike each other intensely, yet still be able to swear eternal love and kiss passionately. A real kiss in an unreal situation.)

Despite my cajoling and explaining, Komaki would not kiss Toshi properly and could not see the difference from the audience's point of view; her argument was that they would believe in the kiss anyway. I pointed out that it severely limited the physical circumstances in which the kiss could take place – the freedom of the actor on the receiving end for a start, never mind hers on the giving; that it restricted the relationship to one or two possibilities. For example, they could not fall over the sofa and roll on the floor in a passionate love-hungry embrace. I didn't win.

(Strangely enough I came across this technique once again in January 2013. Marcus Boyson, playing Mark Rothko in my Hamburger Kammerspiele production of John Logan's *Rot* (*Red*) was using his thumbs to kiss Ken – Jacob Matschke – on the cheek. It was visible from the front rows. This time I won. What is it about thumbs?)

Tokyo has altered radically since that first experience, so much so that there are now two McDonalds sandwiching – or bunning and bapping – the temple in the high street of Kamakura, and the average height of the Japanese has increased five centimetres. The sad thing about theatre in Japan is that, in an attempt to ape the West, it has all but abandoned its cultural roots. There are so many English directors working in Tokyo that it's like an offshoot of the West End. At one point in the Spring of 1998 there were David Leveaux, Glen Walford, Giles Block, Nick Hytner, Stephen Berkoff, John Caird, Gerard Murphy, Robert Ackerman and myself all in town at the same time. The same few authors and plays are re-cycled with regular monotony – Chekov, Ibsen, Shakespeare, Pinter, Beckett. There is always a production of *The Cherry Orchard* or *Romeo and Juliet* on somewhere and the actors aspire to Western make-up and wigs. It was a huge battle to convince my actors in both *The Seagull* and the inevitable *Romeo and Juliet* that they should use their own hair – that blonde and red wigs were anathema.

Musicals are big, monster reproductions of the London or New York originals and audiences for these and straight theatre are mainly female. The stars attract huge salaries and fan clubs. Hordes of women surge down the aisles to throw bouquets on to stage or wait at the stage door to present their loved ones with gifts – the women attracting more attention than the men. One theory is that the dreary frustrated life of the Japanese housewife –

abandoned by the eighteen hour a day Japanese male-machine who comes home late and goes out early – is sublimated by the true romance story of the live theatre; a transference of feeling to real people (the actors) in an unreal situation (the plays) who express in their performance the hopes and fears of the Japanese housewife. A case of total empathy.

The training of the Japanese actor, such as it is, is in pure naturalism. The great theatres of Noh, Kabuki, Bunraku are only practiced by a few companies and, unless an actor specialises in these techniques, then he or she never achieves the most rudimentary training in these forms.

Kabuki is akin to atrophied Restoration theatre, frozen in the eighteenth century and is performed almost solely at the National Theatre, one of the few to receive subsidy.

Kabuki were loose improvised plays, often satirical, based on old stories, rather like Commedia. Then they were topical; now – often meaningless, slow, boring and the reputation rests on the art of the male actor impersonating a female. But, if Kabuki is merely some glorified eighteenth century drag act, then it has totally lost all contact with the reason it came into being in the first place, which was as a popular social antidote to the more formal court drama of Noh. The best thing that could happen to Kabuki is that a group of directors and writers get hold of the form and shake it out, booting it into the twenty first century.

Seeing it, however, at the National theatre, Kokuritsu Gekijo, is an experience.

Once you manage to force your way past the twenty foot flashing Coca Cola sign at the top of the stairs and into the auditorium you are confronted with a vast stage of about thirty metres in width and a long tongue that thrusts out into the audience. Spectators wander in and out, some in traditional dress, and unwrap lunch boxes, eating them noisily during the perform-ance, conversing with their neighbours. From time to time shouts emanate from the audience. Occasionally eight or ten rise spontaneously from their seats and call out something or applaud. Gosh, I thought, this is real audience involvement, true tradition. In the interval, excited, I asked my companion what the people had been shouting. 'They're a professional claque', he said, 'paid to call out the names of the actors when they come on stage or make a special gesture. The richer the actor, the more people he can afford.'

Another example of the commercialisation of tradition, although the precedent of paid claques is a long and historic one. Not so many moons ago, a popular leading player in weekly rep could confidently expect an entrance round of applause from a loyal audience every Monday, no matter what thin disguise he or she cared to adopt for the new play. Their job security perhaps depended on it. In the Restoration theatre, vociferous claques, sometimes hired, cheered their favourites and barracked their rivals as they went along.

The 1830s saw the audiences break up the theatre as Victor Hugo heralded the death of Classicism and the birth of Romanticism in France, when he introduced 'enjambement' – the overlapping line – in *Hernani*. Hugo hired all the artists and poor of the left-bank to cheer him on, but the play never got past the third line and, after five performances, Hugo ran out of money and the play was taken off.

In the 1840's, the French actress Rachel was able to complain to her exhausted *chef de claque* that his efforts in leading the attack – 'three acclamations, four hilarities, two thrilling moments, four renewals of applause and two indefinite explosions' – had disappointed her. In Kabuki theatre today, a hero can be greeted with cries of 'This is what I've been waiting for!' and his rival noisily denounced as 'a radish', all for the price of a few yen. I still believe in the beginning it happened spontaneously.

Noh is something else. This unfathomable ritual of rhythm

and sound is other-worldly. There are six main companies in Tokyo, and on mid-summer's eve a performance takes place at the Haien Shrine in Kyoto. It starts at four in the afternoon and continues until midnight. As the shadows lengthen flaming torches are lit and the performance is played out to the flickering of grotesque shadows. One of the great theatrical experiences.

Noh is a refined ceremony in which movement, dialogue and singing are all rigidly stylised, where the chorus fills a similar role to that in Greek theatre and where the strange combination of musical sounds is designed to transport the spectator into a world of hallucination. These Noh skills are acquired from birth, the actors being born into a family tradition and trained specifically in the form. The director, looking to utilise these traditions in a production in Japan, will look in vain. With a bit of luck an actor or two might have a bit of Ju-jitsu, Kendo or Aikido, but that's about it. Oh yes, and origami.

Performers are expected to be dancers as well as actors and, at the point where the spoken word fails in its power of expression, the language of the dance begins. The actors are placed on a thrust stage close enough to the audience for the intricacy of the dances, the movement, gesticulations, grimaces and poses to be clearly visible. Traditionally Noh performers only rehearse once together before the performance, practicing their roles, music and dance in isolation

Special stage assistants known as 'kurogo', clad in black costumes resembling cassocks, are used to prompt the actors in full view of the audience. (So Erica Eirion prompting Ron Moody in *A Christmas Carol* on stage wasn't so wide of the mark.)

When the costume of an actor becomes disarranged, one of the kurogo quickly rearranges it and attends to the actors head dress. Their job is also to remove any objects from the stage that the actors have dropped or left behind, and after a battle they remove any fallen helmets, weapons or cloaks.

If an actor dies on stage the kurogo holds a black cloth over the corpse and, under cover of the cloth, the 'dead' actor runs off stage. (I dematerialised a 'dead' Juliet from on top of her tomb in the same way.)

When the action requires darkness on stage, the kurogo squats at the actor's feet and illuminates his face with a candle on the end of a long stick. It is from Noh Theatre that Peter Brook took his idea for the single candle at the end of his production of *A Midsummer Night's Dream*.

From that very first experience of *The Seagull* I was sucked into this mysterious world where, at the time, mine was the only white face on the block in a sea of blue suits, white shirts and blouses. At the end of six weeks (so short?) I either had to go home or go native. I felt exactly as John David Morley did in his book *Pictures from the Water Trade*. Beneath the extraordinary politeness, the friendliness, the hospitality (I have five or six wonderful friends from this period), despite the naïve belief that I had come to understand something of the Japanese psyche, something else totally unfathomable was going on. After twenty-five visits I have just abandoned myself to whatever that seductive unfathomable thing is (it's certainly not Buddhism) and enjoy the sensation.

13

The Show Must Go On

The Stage management show report for *Hair*, the Old Vic Theatre, Friday evening 29 October 1993.

'COMMENTS: John Barrowman replaced by Paul Hipp as Claude. Paul Hipp replaced by Colin Peel as Berger. Andree Bernard replaced by Pepsi as Sheila. Felice Arena replaced by Tom Hamilton as Woof. Rebecca Vere replaced by Linda Mae Brewer as Jeannie. Pepsi replaced by Andrea Francis except for Lincoln. Andrea Francis replaced by Clare Coates. Tom Hamilton was replaced by Paul Cloks as Hubert, Adrian Pang as the General and John Wilkes Booth. Carl Anthony was replaced by Colin R. Patterson as Margaret Mead, Adrian Pang as the Crooner, Christopher Novak as the 1,000 year-old monk, Karen Lee Roberts as the Drummer Boy, Andrea Francis as the Dad in the Trip. Paul Darnell was replaced by Adrian Pang. Colin Peel replaced by Sally Ann Barber as the Teacher and the Announcer. Adrian Pang as the Sound Effects man, Christopher Novak with the microphone, Vinette Cowan as the Shooting Soldier and Clare Coates as the Coffin Soldier. Linda Mae Brewer was replaced by Sally Ann Barber as Mum Three and in Black Boys. Marion Springer played Naked Aquarius. All the lifts were cut'.

Friends who saw the show that night rang me and said they had enjoyed it very much. I don't know what it was they enjoyed. It certainly wasn't Hair.

The Show Must Go On

Michael Pennington on *The Wars of the Roses* weekend marathon in Stamford Connecticut USA June 1988.

'Clyde Pollitt had now gone down with full pneumonia and put himself into hospital in New York; while Ian Burford had been attacked by a mystery virus and was unable to move. We looked at the implications of two understudies going on multiplied by seven plays, thankful that we had survived so much of the tour without meeting an emergency like this before. It was a humdinger. *Richard II* and the two *Henry VIs* were not too much of a problem, but on Saturday night we would get to *Henry V* where Ian played Exeter and Clyde the King of France; they had an important scene together, and John Darrell, Oxford, understudied them both. A number of absurd solutions suggested themselves before we settled that John should do Exeter (who carries on into *Henry VI*); but we were thus without a King of France. Chris Hunter, who was already in the French scenes as Orleans, volunteered to learn the fairly-familiar lines, while Ben Bazell went on for Orleans, a smaller part. Chris thus fell in with the grand ESC tradition of busking – daily rep – that I had begun when I went on as Gloucester in Chichester. The next morning, in *Henry VI*, Lancaster, worse still, Ian understudied Clyde as the wicked Bishop of Winchester. Another black hole. Not to be outdone by Chris, I volunteered to learn that one. In this play John Darrell continued as Exeter, doubling with his own part as Sir William Lucy, a role already riddled with quick changes. *Henry VI*, York was less of a problem as long as Andy Jarvis broke off in the middle of Richard Crookback to fill in as Lord Say, who is murdered by Jack Cade's mob, while I had to remember, once I had perished as Cade, to come back almost immediately and perish again as Rutland's Tutor (I died five times in all that Sunday). And so on and on. To shorten a tedious tale, there were over that weekend thirty-two understudy performances (plus the two specially learned). Our understudy system, necessarily imperfect, squeaked and strained, and we came closer than ever to real barnstorming as actors dropped scripts in the wings, rushed on in unfamiliar roles, hoping that someone would guide them off again when they'd finished, and that they could re-find their scripts and sort out their next unscheduled entrance. And all in front of the *New York Times*. Laughably, *Newsweek* was in as well as the *New York Times* – this was the closest we were coming to New York and both journals planned to drop in for a short time on Saturday before heading back to town to cover the Tony Awards. Presumably they would castigate Equity for having let us in. So we blustered on, ranting apprehensively through *Henry IV, Part 2*. At this point I got a message that both *Newsweek* and *The Times* had cancelled their tickets for the Tonys, preferring to stay on with us through Sunday and watch the remainder of our cycle. Something told me that this might not be in order to put the finishing touches to lousy reviews. Jack Kroll (*Newsweek*) rang through on Saturday afternoon and asked for an immediate interview about the company's background to accompany his notice. I did the interview in costume immediately after being crowned as *Henry V*, which I thought would be judicious. The light in his eyes was unmistakable, and both reviews (which happened to come out on my birthday) stand as appeasement's for the many hard times we have had since 1986. We've been quoting them to anyone who'll listen ever since. 'The complete and indispensable Shakespearian even . . . a monumental achieve-ment . . . in New York, as in Stamford (the company) could have its own festival' (*New York Times*); 'An awesome feat of talent and stamina . . . this amazing company achieved the seemingly impossible: they kept the complexity of the epic but made it clear as crystal . . . the rare feat of making Shakespeare sound like real interchanges between real people while keeping the power and glory of the poetry . . . wonderful actors . . . dozens of great performances . . . Bogdanov's inspired strokes . . . make it clear that Shakespeare, done with passion, power and intelligence, is still the hottest ticket in world theatre (*Newsweek*)'.

At what point does the show 'going on' cheat the customer and all concerned? I have romantically always believed in the old adage. In over two hundred and fifty productions I have postponed a first night three times and only on five occasions have I lost previews – three of them in Germany. In eight years on the road, the ESC never lost a single performance in over one thousand five hundred even though at one point, in a ten actor version of *Romeo and Juliet*, both Romeo and Juliet were 'off'. I don't know whether to be proud of this or to kick myself for being such a fool.

The Germans have no such compunction. There is no system of understudies. If somebody is ill, the show is cancelled, or somebody reads the part with a script in the hand. And where the English actor, with pneumonia, three cracked ribs, gout and a broken nose will struggle on to stage with the aid of a zimmer frame, three guide dogs, a drip feed and an oxygen mask – whispering – 'Don't worry about me, chaps, I'll be all right' – the Germans, at the first hint of a bug, head for the nearest consultant, returning with a certificate that states 'no performances for at least a month' and a rest cure in Lanzarote. Jerome Savary, exasperated at the constant Teutonic dental trail, once exploded 'I sink dat ze Germans have sixty-seven teeth!' before disappearing off back to Paris, neglecting to tell his cast, who were waiting in the canteen for the morning rehearsal to continue . . .

If you're going to postpone, really postpone. An actor has a psychological peak to which he or she builds for the opening performance, or premiere, first night etc., and while that peak may be maintained for possibly forty-eight hours, any longer and the energy and the mental preparation nose dive. Sufficient time has to elapse to allow this deflationary trough to occur and for the actors' momentum to build up again. So – at least two weeks.

There is one advantage to postponing though (apart from the obvious one of longer preparation): in so doing you fool the company first night 'cold'. Don't leave it too long, though, or the bugger will get you on the way back.

If a director must weigh carefully the decision to postpone, even more crucial is the decision to abandon. We are too fond of being a hero, too much the romantic. Usually it's a question of economics. We never cancel a show because to do so is to write off a lot of money that we either don't have in the first place or because we need the income. But what happens if we find ourselves in the middle of a production with a sinking feeling that, for whatever reason, it just isn't going to work. German directors have the answer. They just walk out (or postpone endlessly, see above). British directors are afraid – often rightly – of being called irresponsible or of letting people down. Most of the time, however, the only person you let down is yourself – well the whole production and the audience as well. You then struggle to paper over the cracks in an effort to wool-pull over the audiences' and critics' eyes, knowing that you've made an utter bish of the whole thing. Much better to do the decent thing, sometimes (only sometimes, mind).

In an ideal world, where such decisions are not financial but artistic, how many shows would eventually end up in the dustbin, rather than on the stage? Unfortunately, the world is not ideal and we are forced to accept an unequal struggle. But I am more and more convinced that the show does not necessarily have to go on. However, it takes courage for it not to and, where a public paying audience is concerned, I'm glad of the British understudy system.

. . .

Never open a show just after Christmas. Best to put as much distance between yourself and Mr Whiskers as possible. Christmas festivities are another mind sapping exercise, soaking up energy like blotting paper. It isn't the excess of stomach fillers that causes actors to creep unwillingly to school. It's the whole thing. I know, because I've done it twice and suffered the consequences. One was not my fault.

I directed a fairly anarchic version of *The Hunchback of Notre Dame* by Ken Hill for the Cottesloe at the Royal National Theatre Christmas 1977. The previews were a riot (as was the run) but, as with a lot of physically based audience participation shows, it was fairly sprinting up the finishing straight having struggled round the final bend. Peter Hall, whose experience of these kind of shows was fairly negligible, thought that it wasn't going to make it in time to the finishing tape, and panicked.

He took the decision to postpone, deciding that instead of opening on 21st December, the premiere should take place a week later after Christmas on 28th December. Disaster.

As it happened, the preview on what should have been the first night was a triumph, the second date as leaden as the left over Christmas pud. It didn't stop Peter sneaking in at the back most nights though to see Morag Hood as Esmerelda chased through the audience, who often aided her by retaining the pursuing soldiers captive, sometimes holding them down and sitting on them. On one occasion Morag was hauled up to the balcony by a pair of braces that two thoughtful gentlemen dangled down for her to hold on to. And Peter's kids would greet him every breakfast morn with a dawn chorus of the brothel song from *Hunchback* – 'Bums, tits, bums, tits, having it away . . .' (Not my words) It was their favourite show. Adults being rude. I must remind Edward and Rebecca some time. . . .

Conversely the ill-fated David Essex musical *Mutiny*! in 1986 should have had a much longer postponement. Bill Dudley had designed an all singing, all dancing, teas-made boat that was far too big to fit into the Piccadilly Theatre and the ten days technical time allotted to mount the show were patently not enough.

To begin with, the foundations of the stage had to be

excavated to a depth of some twenty feet to accommodate the central hydraulic shaft, which was then set in concrete. In the event the workmen drilled through a Victorian sewer, two power cables and a gas main before striking oil. To say that we were delayed is to put it mildly. Howard Panter, the producer, postponed the first night by a week, leaving us with just six previews. The show was booked out for two months and we could easily have left the opening a couple more weeks. It wouldn't have affected the attendance.

For the boat had a life of its own.

It could tilt backwards and forwards, from side to side, go up and down, split in the middle and, by virtue of traversing, revolve and, if desired, do all of these things at the same time. The problem was that, out of control, it smashed into flats, walls, people, grinding to a stop for hours on end as we repaired the damage. Not to mention hydraulic hiccups. Richard Bullimore, the production manager, would say 'When it's up and running, you'll forget this ever happened.' Ho, ho.

It was a technical monster crying out to be conquered. I refused to accept that the boat could not be materialised from a bare stage at the opening of the show. The deck, when the boat was down in the bowels, was the boarded stage with the monster secreted down below in the depths. To have begun with the boat already visible would have been to give away our secret weapon.

I battled with it for five days. Howard wanted to give up and start with the company already on the boat. I refused to give in, finally solving the problem by revolving the stage clockwise instead of anti-clockwise as it was designed to do, with the entire crew forcibly dragging seven tons of iron rigging three feet upstage as it flew in, at the same time anchoring the rigging over a spigot and clamping it off to the sides of the boat as it revolved, an exercise that cost many a knuckle. It required split-second timing. There were just a couple of seconds when rigging and spigot could coincide as the boat revolved and traversed. When it worked it was the most stunning effect, Bill's boat spiralling up out of the mist from a bare stage.

And once you were on it there was no getting off – or on – there was a sheer drop of thirty feet on either side. First Mate Tony Carpenter was ten minutes late one night and he couldn't board until the interval. The cast improvised around his absence.

For a whole month I stood on a strip of stage at the front barely one metre wide, orchestrating the bastard. Twenty-four hours a day, a bottle of Jameson Whiskey at the ready. Whenever I watched the show afterwards, I would cynically measure the mechanical effects in terms of the number of days in my life it had taken to achieve them.

Five days to materialise the boat, three days to de-materialise it. Four days to turn the stage into Tahiti, three days to get rid of it. I only managed to solve the problem of bringing the Tahitian canoe up from the depths, fully manned, and shuttle it to the back of the stage on the afternoon of the day we opened to the press.

A further two or three weeks were needed to work on the book, lyrics, music, performances . . . the first night was a triumph of eyes, tits and teeth over fear. I don't believe that even with a further postponement that we would have taken the critics with us, but at least we would have been in with a chance. I collapsed with jaundice after the experience, the hardest thing I have ever done in my life. It cost me my liver. Imagine after all that, waking up and reading Michael Coveney in the *Financial Times* 'This production is staggeringly inept'. The little shit.

14

Saving One's Bacon

The first time I warmed to Peter Hall was when I realised that at heart he was really nothing but a pie and chips man. The day before I had read in a magazine supplement one of those vacuous 'A Room in the Day Life and Food Style of How I met My Favourite Dog' articles, in which Peter had stated that his preferred method of relaxation was eating Japanese food with his 'then' wife, Maria Ewing. And here he was, Monday lunch time, ahead of me in the queue at the National Theatre canteen, casting a cold eye on the bean sprout salad, downing his thumb at the smoked fish and coleslaw, turning his nose up at the cottage cheese and assorted nuts, and homing in on a giant sized plateful of Le Pie de Porc Pommes Frites.

I know the feeling well. It comes upon you the two weeks before opening night, this irresistible urge to stuff your face full of stodge – pies, sandwiches, bacon butties, sausage rolls, chips – the body crying out for energy and carbohydrate, the craving akin to being quad pregnant. The curse of the eighteen-hour directorial day, chained to a blackened auditorium, is the unhealthy diet. Eating on the run. The signs are the plastic cartons on the production desk, heavy with the mouldering remnants of burst teabags, cigarette butts and toffee papers. The stack of grease-grained cardboard plates with the remnants of five days fish and chips, Mars Bar wrappers and orange peel. Directors either have stomachs lined with cast iron and ferrous concrete or nurse a volcanic peptic ulcer. It is not an uncommon sight to hear a director, after an all-nighter, the body contorted, bent double at ninety degrees, the left hand clutching the stomach, the right a carton of milk, a face full of pain like a pug in labour, order a toasted bacon and egg sarnie, two rounds of fried bread, black pudding and beans to wash down the Rennies.

In an effort to beat the belly, I tried reversing this unnatural order of eating. At the beginning of rehearsal I now go on a diet. I'm accustomed to working right through the day without stopping. My actors and stage management team get their statutory breaks, but I find that once I begin I want to carry on. Any gap in a ten or twelve hour day and I lose concentration. And if I eat I go to sleep. So I drink tea, common or garden or herbal, depending on my mood, an intravenous drip feed to my right hand. And eat fruit. Apples. (Lately it hasn't managed to keep the doctor away). This has the effect of keeping the head and body clear and I lose weight. Of course, I then blow it all at midnight with a bloody great meal which then lies heavy on the stomach. We can't all be perfect. The object of this spartan food-frust is to build up a resistance to the mental and physical pressure that starts to exert itself in the closing stages of technical rehearsals when a small cloven-hoofed voice whispers in your ear, prodding your guts with its fork – 'How about a sausage sarnie, eh? Or a nice pork pie? You likes those . . .'

The theatre canteen is a constant object of thespian criticism and, for an artistic director, is the theatrical equivalent of the bicycle shed syndrome. (Meetings in Hamburg of the Betriebsrat – the theatre advisory and complaints council, the union – were regular battle grounds for the problems of pedal-power parking.) The theatre canteen can sometimes be the direct descendant of that post-war Puritan culinary disaster – the British restaurant – the fare on offer often only marginally one gag up from powdered eggs, condensed milk and spam fritters. It is the one area that Egon Ronay or the *Good Food Guide* haven't yet dared to tackle. It is not that all of them are necessarily bad; it is the familiarity of the fat-fried fare that breeds indigestion. Faced with an unending combination of Mediterranean lookalikes, British oddities (very odd – 'Bean Sprout Lasagne with a Cooly [*sic*] of Pureed Lettuce') and the odd special (odder still) the most hardened foodie could be forgiven for turning Brahmin. Even Joachim Ziemmans (Thomas Mann's *The Magic Mountain*) complained after ten months in the Berghof sanatorium about the five meals a day, the menus of which would have done justice to Hester Blumenthal. What hope then for yesterday's Cottage Pie re-cycled as Bolognaise Sauce au Gratin or Cod Fillets and Vegetable Pie, turned Fish Cake and Ratatouille?

I once wrote a revue for the Belfast festival entitled *Baked Beans and Cold Rice Pudding* the opening number of which was a song of that name with music by John Gould:

'Baked beans and cold rice pudding –
Tomato Ketchup and custard –
Jam sponge and old fish fingers –
Mangy mince meat – covered in marmalade –
Remind me of you'.

Or of most theatre canteens in the world.

At the Abbey Theatre, Dublin, the actors used to have written into their contract that they would perform in so many plays a year that included a meal on stage during the course of the action, a supplement to their meagre wage. Tea and biscuits didn't count. Have a look at O'Casey's *Juno and the Paycock* – 'Eat your sassidge'.

'Cockles and lava bread, mussels and mullet,
These are a few of my favourite things.'
and are to be found in abundance at Swansea market. Non-

Waleans are continually flummoxed by the nomenclature 'bread' for what turns out to be a black, green, slimy, pulped mass of seaweed culled from the mud flats around Penclawdd on the Gower peninsular. Penclawdd – ponies and cattle grazing the marsh. Mist and manure. But mixed with oats, fried with bacon, butter and garlic, placed on toast with fresh cockles as big as old pennies for topping, lava bread is one of the world's great feasts.

Since launching the Wales Theatre Company in 2003 I've now done a total of fifteen shows at the wonderful Swansea Grand Theatre, the best of the renovated theatres in which to work in the whole of the British Isles, the audiences veering wildly between standing room only and running on empty in Dylan Thomas's homely, welcoming, ugly lovely, town.

However, the most important cultural asset that Swansea possessed at one time was not the Grand Theatre, not its music festival, not the Morriston Orpheus Choir, not even Dylan T. No, not one of those things. What Swansea had, par excellence, was a representative of those rapidly disappearing, oak-aged establishments, a theatre pub. (Changed now, utterly). By that, I mean one which, when, at eleven p.m., the normal clientele is being politely evicted on its ear, the weary thespian, exhausted from the day's honest toil, the honest sweat coursing down the honest brow, is welcomed into the pub bar with open arms.

'The Singleton'.

It was little appreciated in legal circles before extended opening hours that the theatre, with its working day of sometimes fourteen hours, needs a place communally to relax for an hour or so at the end of it all. To sit back, wind down, release a different kind of energy over a few jars: to tell each other a few home truths, to set the world to rights, to curse the director, to mutually admire, to tear the set, the management, the theatre, the publicity officer, the dressing rooms, the programme, the front of house facilities to pieces. And then to fall out into the night for a vindaloo chop suey pizza before getting six hours, head down and doing it all again on the morrow.

Mind you, I'm not the first frequenter of The Singleton who, after a couple of glasses of wine on an empty stomach, on being confronted by a small white pig with black spots snuffling its way underneath the crowded tables, has rushed out into the night swearing eternal teetotalism. Daisy was a regular nocturnal visitor to the bar (no dogs allowed – pigs optional, courtesy of the Landlord) devouring an enormous quantity of crisps – cheese and onion, salt and vinegar, bacon – it's all one to them or her. (Mrs Butcher Beynon to her husband as she feeds the cat under the table – 'She likes the liver, Ben'. 'She ought to, Bess, it's her brother's'. That was written in Swansea. Someone else with a touch of DTs – Dylan Thomas). How does Old Spot Daisy know that packet of crunchy crispy crackling isn't some near or distant relative?

Dublin had a famous one too, opposite the Gate Theatre, Grooms. Also gone alas. It was the headquarters of the Fianna Fail Party and frequented by politicians, artists and lawyers alike. Paddy Groom would greet a green and raiding six foot six Garda Siochana recruit, fresh up from the country and making a name for himself at 2.00 a.m. in the morning, with the words 'Ah, come in, Sergeant. What are you having – a drink or a transfer?'

I was once carousing there circa 1.00 a.m. when one such recruit pushed his way into the full to bursting room and in a strong Kerry accent began to question the residential credentials of the clientele, inscribing the while in his little black book.

'Name please?'

'Norman Rodway.'

'Profission?'

'Ac-tor.'

'Name please?'

'Godfrey Quigley.'

'Profission?'

'Ac-tor.'

'Name please?'

'Lord Chief Justice Donagh MacDonagh and I hardly think we'll meet again.'

Time to go! It's throwing up time. Time to fortify the seventy four inner man with some carrot juice and corn bread ready for the 6.00 a.m. lighting session. Or better still, a nice pork pie. You likes them . . . doesn't you Peter?

15

The Romans in Britain

The furore over the RSC's production of *The Marat Sade* in 2011 is a timely reminder of how dilatory theatre has been in fulfilling its obligation to engage and challenge. Over the past twenty years or so mainstream theatre has been brainwashed into thinking that a diet of musicals and technologically inspired design can substitute for ideological engagement. David Hare soft pink porn has been about as radical as we have got, give or take Sarah Kane, as theatre has rushed to try and compete with TV and Film for an audience. The passion and politics unleashed by the abolition of censorship are a dim and distant memory. That was BC. Before Cats

'*Homo sum: Humani nihil a me alienum puto*' – 'I am a man: nothing human is alien to me . . .' (Terence), but some things are deemed more alien than others. Morality is what the majority at any particular moment happen to like and immorality is what they dislike. It is a question of context. There is a shifting point of acceptability dependent on the *moeurs* and mores of the day. It is the nature of art to push those points further and further along a line of universal acquiescence. The representatives of what Stallybrass and White (*Politics and Poetics of Transgression*, Routledge, 1986) define as the 'High discourses – literature, philosophy, statecraft, the language of the church and the university' have again and again taken the decision as to what is appropriate for the public at large (even when the public simply equates with the educated middle-class).

Until the abolition of his powers in 1968, the Lord Chamberlain's office exercised a fairly strict system of censorship and, as Alan Sinfield comments, 'as long as the makers and audiences of theatre were broadly at one with the dominant values in society, this caused little problem . . . but the new movement (of the 60s) perceived at once that censorship tended to privilege and legitimate traditional ideology and to suppress its own'. Plays such as Edward Bond's *Saved*, with its analysis of teenage violence (the 'baby stoning' episode), Arthur Miller's *A View from the Bridge*, with its homosexual overtones, challenged the structures of the Lord Chamberlain and, via the medium of private, members-only club performances, (such as those of the Royal Court's Theatre Upstairs and the Arts Theatre), were able to by-pass his control.

But the abolition of censorship has not meant that any play can be produced anywhere in Britain. The Establishment has accommodated playwrights whose works are a challenge to the dominant ideology but the cultural product is only acceptable if that challenge is contained within certain limits.

How far can you go? I found out in 1980. Peter Hall invited me to join the National Theatre and, as my first production, asked me to read a new play by Howard Brenton, which he was enthusiastic about, *The Romans in Britain*. The play is highly political – an attack on imperialism and a parallel is made with the British in Northern Ireland. It is also highly moral, asking us as a nation to consider our stance on torture, rape and human rights. In many ways the play was ahead of its time (if that can that ever be the case in a play about invading forces) for the advent of torture, rape and violence that were to follow in Rawanda, Bosnia, Iraq, Syria etc., as men (and women) descended to the level of beasts in their perpetration of crimes against humanity cast Howard's play in an entirely different light.

I thought the first half in particular contained some of the best new writing I had come across in a long time. Peter and I agreed that the problems were with the second half, which appeared like another play (indeed the two halves had been written as separate playlets). The language was hard and explicit (the play is about an invading force, the Romans, in 54 BC, the British in Northern Ireland 1980) and one of the central scenes is the attempted male rape of a young Celt by a Roman soldier, a metaphor for the rape of one culture by another.

I staged the scene uncompromisingly, centre stage, in the bright white light of the mid-day sun. It was shocking, but it was meant to be. The issues were confronted, not fudged. After seeing a run-through of the play in its late stages Peter and Christopher Morahan questioned Howard and myself on the wisdom of the staging. Could it be set upstage, in the leafy shadows behind one of the large trees constituting the forest clearing. We replied that to do so would make the scene more salacious and titillating and would be dodging the issue – as if we were afraid of the most important scene in the play, its central metaphor. Peter and Christopher both accepted the argument, agreeing that it was fully justified in the context. After that Peter stood by the play, the production, myself, in every way, fronting the press and media, making the case for the freedom of the arts. He is a giant of our times.

However . . . the facts. *The Romans in Britain* opened in the Olivier Theatre October 16th, 1980. Mary Whitehouse, President of the National Viewers and Listeners Association applied to the Attorney General, Sir Michael Havers, to have the play taken off under the *Obscene Publications Act*. She was refused. She then applied for permission under *The Theatres Act*. Permission was again refused. Both these are civil statutes.

Her lawyers then found a loophole in the 1956 *Sexual Offences Act*, whereby it is a criminal offence to procure an act of gross indecency in a public place. It was a law introduced in the wake of the Wolfenden Report on Homosexuality, designed to stop such occurrences as soliciting in public lavatories. This law, Mary Whitehouse and her solicitors applied to the stage, and I was prosecuted as director of the play as the person being responsible for the arranging of the scene of attempted rape. I was the 'procurer', the scene was the 'gross indecency'. The Attorney General argued that he was powerless to stop the case which was being brought under criminal law by a private citizen. The trial took place at the Old Bailey, March 1982.

As it happened I had one previous conviction. The date 1961 when I was at the University of Trinity College, Dublin. It was the occasion of the 21st birthday celebration of a Welsh college friend Peter Cocks. We had been merrymaking (I use the term loosely) at the Punchbowl at the bottom of Chatham Street. Being evicted at the unholy hour of 11 o'clock and refused re-admission to answer the bellow of nature, I retreated round the corner of the Del Rio chip shop (alas no more). In the midst of my meditation I felt a heavy hand on my shoulder and, thinking it was Cocksy messing about, I turned round and pissed all over the boots of a 6ft 6 Garda Siochana, (Irish Police). 'You're under arrest', he understated in broad Kerry. At the time, although still a student, I was appearing in a late night revue at the Pike Theatre – *Still Crackers*. (It was my first professional engagement. We were on shares. The first week it was one shilling and seven pence, the second – ninepence ha'penny, the third – thruppence or a packet of crisps. I took the crisps.) I explained to the Garda that I had to be on stage at midnight and he stepped into the road and flagged down a passing Mini, crammed to the maxi, and said to the driver – 'I have to charge your man here with indecent exposure. Would you ever give us a lift down to Pearce Street Gards Station'. Six of us in that Mini (or seven if you count the Garda as two) was the second cousin to the 'how many elephants can you get in a telephone box' joke. I was duly charged and the Duty Sergeant kindly gave me a lift up to the Pike Theatre and stayed to watch the show.

When the case came to court, Lord Chief Justice Donagh MacDonagh (himself a playwright) asked me 'Do you have anything to say in your defence?' 'Yes', I said, 'I deplore the lack of public conveniences in Dublin'. He laughed. 'So do I. Fined five shillings. Next case please.'

* * *

During the rehearsals of *Romans* word went out that alleged hardcore sex was being performed by the actors under my direction. The theatre's ushers planned a boycott. To scotch any false rumours, I invited the entire staff of the National Theatre to an open rehearsal and supplied a barrel of Fullers beer for the occasion. Amid much post performance revelry, the audience gave the performers and the play, including the controversial scene an overwhelming thumbs up. (A prescient term as will be later revealed.)

The affair was not without its humourous side. Charlie Hanson, my assistant, rehearsing the scene in question in the minute hospitality room at the National Theatre, turning the bust of George Bernard Shaw to the wall . . . putting a hat over the face of the bust of Lord Olivier . . . a painter on the roof of Rehearsal Room One watching the scene in amazement, his brush mechanically daubing white paint over the plate glass. Greg Hicks, cycling home, seeing a billboard – 'Sex Play Rocks West End', turning the paper over and seeing a picture of himself doing the rocking. A letter from a Colonel overseas. 'I don't know who you are, Sir, or what you do, but I'm with you. Please find enclosed cheque for £5.' Diminutive Yvonne Bryceland, on her first entrance, wrestling to control three huge Irish wolfhounds, their leashes held in one hand. Melvyn Bedford snoring on stage in the corn, missing his cue . . .

In October, *The Romans in Britain* began to preview. From the start the opening line of the play in the Olivier Theatre was greeted by an outbreak of surprised titters, sharp in-drawing of breath and the occasional loud guffaw. It was seen immediately by some as a direct assault on the bourgeois assumption that all the words uttered on that piece of hallowed board should conform to certain unwritten rules of literary acceptability, or as a direct criticism of the National Theatre itself as an elite representative of privileged culture.

> The edge of a forest at night. Against the night sky the forest looks like a black cliff.
> Silence.
> Then in the distance dogs bark. It is just past midnight on August 27th, 54 BC.
> We are fifty miles north of the River Thames.
> In the trees someone stifles a cry.
> Then out of the trees, come two figures. One is a big man, Daui, with big head and big hands, the other a small man, Conlag, quick and ferret like. They are in rags. Their skin is weathered and filthy. The small man clutches a large, leather bag. He looks about him, then speaks.
>
> CONLAG: Where the fuck are we?
>
> DAUI: Day in day out, lying in a boat with salt round the back of my eyeballs. In a river up to my neck. Marshes with leeches. Moors with birds of prey. Rocks with wildcats. In sun, in rain, in snow – I have heard you ask, where the fuck are we.
>
> CONLAG: Well, Where are we?
>
> DAUI: How the fuck do I know?

The gauntlet was later to be picked up by numerous knights and suits in shiny grey when the play arrived at the scene of attempted homosexual rape. At the penultimate preview, a specially invited guest night, the (then) Conservative leader of the Greater London Council (GLC), Sir Horace Cutler, (where is he now?), led a walk out of forty councillors. He sent a telegram to Peter Hall, who was in New York at the time opening *Amadeus*, threatening to withdraw the National Theatre's grant, and then released the contents of his telegram to *The Evening News* and *The Daily Mirror*. A deliberate, calculated, political act. The consequences were that later the Cottesloe was closed for about six months. The ball was rolling.

We opened to mixed reviews, ranging from a disparaging 'These ignoble Romans are a national disgrace' in *Now* magazine, to discussions of the play's political content. Only one thing remained constant, the shock of the attempted rape scene. Its effect was later compared by one reviewer to that of the news of John F Kennedy's assassination.

Tipped off by a journalist, Mary Whitehouse, an indefatigable campaigner for censorship, who wished to rid TV of anything distasteful (ie anything that she didn't like), somewhat exaggeratedly and hysterically maintained, even though she had not seen *Romans* herself, that it would 'over stimulate' men and incite them to bugger young boys. She refused to see the play as she was too frightened it would lead to the 'corruption of her soul', so she requested the Metropolitan Police to examine whether the play was 'an offence against the Theatres Act of 1968' which outlawed performances 'likely to deprave or corrupt.' In her diary she wrote – 'Three Roman soldiers are apparently tearing off all their clothes and raping three young male Britons in full view of the audience!' Further –

'It has been known for two thousand years how the Romans – some of them – behaved in Britain. We haven't needed to wait all those years for the National Theatre to come and show us'.

Once again Mary Whitehouse wrote in her diary – 'For a woman of seventy one, a mother and a grandmother, to challenge an act of simulated buggery at the National Theatre . . . what a comment on the times in which we live.'

On the night of December 19th I was in the green-room having a drink after the performance with Howard, Greg and

Michael Bryant (Julius Caesar) when I was called to the stage door. A small, mousey man in glasses stood there with a letter in his hand, smiling.

'Are you Michael Bogdanov? I have something for you,' he announced.

'Thank you!' I replied, taking the letter, thinking that this smiley man was a fan after an autograph . . . it was Ross-Cornes, Mary Whitehouse's solicitor. As I went back upstairs I opened the letter. It was a writ.

Howard Brenton: 'Bullied by Whitehouse, the police visited the National's production of *The Romans in Britain* three times. They found there were no grounds, under the laws that govern public decency in entertainment, to prosecute. Everything went quiet. The play was doing well, the production was getting better and better. Then one night Michael Bogdanov, the director, and I were having a celebratory drink with the actors in the green room. Peter Hall had just extended the play to a second season. A call came: someone was at the stage door for Michael. It was Whitehouse's solicitor with a writ. Wham! The strobe lights were blasting at us again. Whitehouse's lawyers had spent a couple of months going through the laws of Olde England to come up with a bizarre way of prosecuting not me, the play's maker, but its director, under the Sexual Offences Act. They claimed he was a pimp because he had cast the actors. This nasty little legal manoeuvre made Michael's life hell for a year.'

And so it began. A first it seemed like a joke and all and sundry treated the affair frivolously. Then suddenly things became much more serious. After three preliminary hearings at Horseferry Magistrates Court (sometimes you would think that the Law Chariot has square wheels) I was committed to trial and a date was set for March 1982 at the Old Bailey. The Examining Magistrate, Mr. Harrington, apologised for his judgement saying 'It appears illogical, but I must interpret the law as it stands and not as it might have been. I think it absurd that had Mr. Bogdanov been a woman director he would have no case to answer, but as it stands that appears to be the law and I must interpret it as it stands'.

The law was (is) more than an ass. The press had a field-day with the judgement. Had I been Michelle Bogdanov, as one pointed out, I could with impunity have arranged scenes of attempted buggery till the cows came home. Although only I was charged at this point it was expected that both Peter and Greg would be called to give evidence, and if I were convicted, both actors would be tried and fined. I faced up to three years in jail.

It was at this point that Geoffrey Robertson, the Junior on the case, wrote to the Attorney General, Sir Michael Havers, a Conservative government appointment, asking him to enter a *nolle prosequi* – a measure whereby he can take over a case himself and drop it if he thinks it is not in the public interest. This he refused to do. He said he was powerless to stop the prosecution going forward as it was a criminal offence but wanted us to know that he did 'not lack courage where Mrs. Whitehouse is concerned'. Ho, Ho!

John Smythe – a committed Christian barrister employed by Whitehouse to prosecute *Gay News* for blasphemy over James Kirkup's 'queer Jesus' poem, 'The Love that Dares to Speak its Name' – was briefed to probe into the actors' sexuality. Greg Hicks was asked whether he became aroused during the scene and whether he found it necessary afterwards to masturbate in the wings. As neither thought had ever previously occurred to him, it was an indication of the unpleasant tactics that the other side might use.

Lord Hutchinson, once wedded to Peggy Ashcroft, and a redoubtable defender of Free Speech (what would he make of Levenson?) acted for my defence, assisted by Geoffrey Robertson, as junior defence counsel. The Judge, Christopher Staughton (recreations given in *Who's Who* as Bridge and Dahlia growing), was chosen, it was rumoured, on the grounds that he was believed to be knowledgeable on laws pertaining to sodomy. In fact, he was an expert on Maritime Law, or Bottomry as it is called – so, if the rumour were true, one can see how perversely and idiotically the association with *Romans* was made. Smythe, the original prosecution lawyer, probably sensing that the case was fraught with difficulties, suddenly retired from the brief, allegedly suffering from a mysterious virus and Ian Kennedy QC, now a high court judge, took his place.

On the Saturday night before the trial was due to take place, there was a reading of the play, led by Howard, on the empty stage of The Old Vic. I was not allowed anywhere near the theatre on the grounds that we did not wish to give the opposition any ammunition with which to shoot me. Geoffrey Robertson, who attended, had left his papers for the trial in his briefcase in his car outside in The Cut. The car was broken into and the briefcase stolen. Panic – the entire preparation for my defence had gone. The next day it was returned to him by a policeman. It had been found abandoned in the street, the papers intact, my life of no commercial value whatsoever.

I arrived at the court innocently looking something like a 70s porn star – long hair, black leather jacket, two gold chains and a medallion over a black roll neck sweater. I would have convicted me straight away. The public gallery was packed with critics, press, public, anti and pro, but was significant for one notable absence – Mary Whitehouse. She had chosen to stay at home and pray she said. The jury, most of whom looked like they had never been to the theatre before (maybe I'm being unfair), already seemed bemused at the legal jargon pertaining to homosexuality, the law and the theatre, and the red-tops, all present and incorrect, were having a salacious field-day with the case, preying on the then fear that the floodgates of homosexuality were about to be opened via a 'luvvies' loophole.

We had an impressive array of witnesses lined up to take the stand among whom Sir Trevor Nunn, Janet Suzmann, Peter Brook, Lord Goodman, John Mortimer, with Lord Laurence Olivier waiting in the wings, should Herr Staughton allow their evidence as admissible, which on his showing up to then was dubious.

The trial began with a three hour discussion as to whether I should be allowed bail and live at home rather than spend my nights for the duration of the trial incarcerated as a common criminal in the cells beneath the Old Bailey. Lord Hutchinson finally managed to persuade Judge Staughton that I was no danger to society, was not about to flee to America and face extradition, and Staughton grudgingly allowed me my freedom. It was a measure of how ill-equipped he was to handle a trial of this nature. Back to Bottomry, m'Lud.

The preliminaries, sorting out the protocol and the parameters of the trial, took up three days. On the third day, the turning point of the trial arrived.

Geoffrey Robertson, on a hunch, produced a seating plan of the Olivier Theatre and Hutchinson asked Ross-Cornes, Mary Whitehouse's only witness, her solicitor, to mark where he had been sitting. He borrowed Staughton's pen and marked a cross on the sheet. Hutchinson looked at it. Ross Cornes had been sitting at the back of the Circle, some ninety feet away from the point of impact so to speak.

'The back row! You sat in the back row – the cheapest seats in the house? Mrs. Whitehouse couldn't afford the front stalls? You go to the theatre knowing that your task is to collect evidence for a very serious prosecution of my client, a man who has never committed a single offence in his life, on a very nasty charge and you sit in the back row?! Do you – can you swear on oath to his Lordship and to the jury that you are certain that you saw the tip of a penis from a distance of ninety feet from the stage?'

The exchange that followed went something like this:–

'Of course, what else could it have been?'

'What would you say if I were to tell you that what you thought was a penis was a thumb?'

'What?'

'Look, man, look!'

Lord Hutchinson demonstrated exactly what Peter Sproule the actor had been doing – bunching his fist up and hitting the inside of Greg Hick's thigh with his thumb.

Gotcha!

Ian Kennedy, turned to his Junior, astonished, with a question on his lips. The Junior spread his hands and shrugged, a look of wide-eyed 'I don't know, this is the first I've heard of it' desperation on his face. Kennedy stood up and said 'I wish for a short adjournment'. Out he strode and the court could hear a row on the phone in the corridor. Kennedy returned.

Stopping the case at a risk to his own career he said,

'I wish to cease the prosecution and I wish the court to understand that I am doing this of my own accord, not on the wishes of my client. The consequences of conviction – irrespective of penalty – would greatly damage Mr. Bogdanov in his personal and professional life.'

He realised he'd been sold a pig in a poke . . . or a poke of a thumb in a thigh.

Judge Staughton (what a card!) had other ideas however. He made three rulings:

1. The *Sexual Offences Act* could not be applied to the stage.

2. A simulated act could still amount to gross indecency.

3. The motive of 'sexual gratification' did not have to be proved for the offence to stand.

In his weasely wisdom he ruled that I still had a case to answer and wished to commit me to a full trial. He denounced Kennedy's decision to withdraw the case without having consulted him,

Judge Christopher Staughton, as 'misconceived and improper'. He said 'once the prosecution has called its evidence a trial must continue'. Kennedy, bravely, maintained his right as the prosecution council to cease a trial at any point if he considers it a waste of time and the public purse. We called in the Attorney General to sort out the mess.

Sir Michael Havers was furious. Such a thing was highly unusual in legal history, but there was nothing for it but to cease the trial forthwith and invoke that legal rarity – a *nolle prosequi*, the very thing that Geoffrey Robertson had asked him to consider all those months ago. Technically I hadn't actually been acquitted, but it was obviously no longer in the public interest to pursue the hearing at the Central Criminal Court. It was a victory of sorts, as Mary Whitehouse, or rather her band of Christian Soldiers, had to pay all the costs. It was highly frustrating that I didn't have the opportunity to put the artistic case for the scene (see below) but I felt a sense of vindication, glad that after eighteen months of uncertainty it was all over.

There followed backstage at the Old Bailey an event, hotly disputed by Geoffrey Robertson, that has gone down in the annals of legal anecdotes. Hutchinson in the ante-chamber volunteered to demonstrate the action for the Attorney General. 'Geoffrey will you be buggered or shall I?' Down on all fours. Gowns and wigs and all. Havers gravely inspecting, Hutchinson banging away at Geoffrey's thigh with his bunched up fist and thumb. Anatomically impossible. Buggery, my arse.

There were many heroes. John Goodwin, press genius of the National, not sleeping, never off the phone. Deflecting, advising, shielding me from the worst excesses. Howard Brenton, my friend, who had written a beautiful and deeply moving play. Touring the country with a one-man reading to raise money. Andrew Leigh, my erstwhile administrator at the Leicester Haymarket Theatre, organising a Theatre Defence Fund. Nicholas

Kent, dramatising the daily events of the trial at the Tricycle Theatre. Sir Peter Hall, who stood firmly in the front line of fire. Believing in the play, believing in the production. The debt that theatre and new writing owe him is immeasurable. The whole of the National Theatre. And of course Lord Hutchinson, freedom-fighter from way back.

There were plenty of villains, not least Christopher Staughton who was too cowardly to dismiss the case despite the glaring anomaly and incongruity of applying this section of criminal law to a piece of theatre. Sir Horace Cutler leader of the Conservative controlled GLC, who staged the walk-out at the preview. The Attorney General. Ah . . . the Attorney General – Michael Havers, actor Nigel Havers' father. Refusing Mary Whitehouse permission to prosecute under the *Theatres Act*; refusing her permission to prosecute under the *Obscene Publications Act*; granting permission under the *Sexual Offences Act* of 1956. The charge? Procuring an act of gross indecency between one man and another. On the stage of the Olivier Theatre. In a play called *The Romans in Britain*, by Howard Brenton. A surreal reality. Refusing to intervene until reluctantly forced to. (His son, the actor Nigel was one of a very few who refused to sign a letter of support for me, organised by the Theatre Defence Fund.) Mary Whitehouse, the night the trial finished, unwilling to give in despite public utterances, angrily bursting into a TV studio to which she had not been invited in order to row with Sir Peter Hall on a late night news programme.

And, first and last, the media. Ah, the media . . . distorting, twisting, hounding, salacious, mendacious. And much worse. Was this monster they were describing me? It must have been. After all, there I was in the dock of the Number One Court of the Old Bailey – previous occupier the Yorkshire Ripper, Peter Sutcliffe. I was a pervert. I was absolutely immoral and I was up on a charge of Gross Indecency. Directors like me should be stopped from doing plays because I was promoting homosexuality.

I went on the 6 o'clock News the day the trial finished, being welcomed by David Dimbleby as a hero – 'It was the thumb, wasn't it? he said. I nodded. He called up to the director's box – 'I told you, you owe me five quid!'. Turning to me – 'Now how shall we do this. I'm afraid you're not able to say the word 'penis'. Children watching you see'. Much discussion as to whether 'male member' was acceptable. Apparently not. Panic. The hour was upon us. We discussed my production of *Hiawatha*, which was currently playing at the National Theatre, instead. Absurd.

Pulling over a TV camera during an interview with News at Ten in protest at the aggressive tactics of the interviewer, John Suchet – brother of David. Valerie Singleton, on yet another TV news programme, storming round the studio on discovering that she had been calling me Peter all through the interview. I then went away for a few days with my family to Boulogne, still pursued by photographers, right onto the ferry. Press restraint? Bring it on.

In 2006, to commemorate 25 years since the trial, Mark Lawson even managed to write a radio play for BBC Radio 4 entitled 'The 3rd Soldier Holds His Thighs', where he attributes things I said to others and gives me some of Howard's and Peter Hall's words. He didn't bother to talk to me you see, the person the play is about. The person alive and kicking, 150 miles away down the M4. . . . Said he couldn't find me. . . . The wanker. I found out about the play by accident when I rang Daniel Evans to ask him if he wanted to play Hamlet in Welsh and English for me. How extraordinary, he said, I've just finished a recording of a piece about *The Romans in Britain* in which I play you. Was I pissed off? Think about it.

* * *

I don't think about it much now. At the time, it was like being plucked up in the steel jaws of some puritanical JCB. It is a strange sensation to realise that you are an object of hatred and vilification. We moved soon afterwards and made our telephone number ex-directory. No more abusive phone calls, illiterate, obscene, anonymous letters, threats to get me, get my family, burn my house down, dog turds through the letter box. (Yes, really.) A fire of hatred, the flames fanned by a salivating media, avidly pursuing their favourite English pastime – the sex life of the private citizen. No matter that unemployment was climbing to three and a half million. This was *real* news. The National Theatre puts on a dirty play.

And how did it all come about? Because a small group of self-appointed guardians of the nation's moral conscience chose to break the contract. The contract that binds the theatre experience together. The stage contracts to pretend, the audience contracts to believe that pretence. If either party breaks the contract then there is trouble. You can't really cut off someone's arm on stage. It's against the law. You can't really have sexual intercourse on stage. It's against the law. Theatre is pretence. Illusion. Always. And the audience contracts to suspend its disbelief. If for one moment the audience stops believing that it is watching three young Celts in 55 BC and sees only three naked actors in 2013 – or 1980 as it was then – then the contract is broken. No proper analysis of the scene, of the play, of the issues can take place. Because reality has been confused with illusion. A scene that starts as a serious exploration of imperialism and examines the behaviour of an invading force, is no longer a metaphor for the rape of a culture. It has become entangled (in the public's mind – and the law) with the view that the playwright, the director and the cast are encouraging the public at large to all run out in to the streets and bugger each other.

John Osbourne, letter to the Guardian. 'I don't go to the theatre to see a lot of buggery. We get quite enough of that at home.'

One cannot escape the feeling that the greatest crime would have been not to put the play on (there was concurrently running at the Royal Court Theatre Upstairs where the naked genitals of a man were threatened with a broken bottle and a girl raped), but that (a) the subject was male rape (had it been female rape, different criteria would have been applied in our sexually hypo-critical society) and (b) that it took place on the Olivier stage, one of the last large scale bastions of bourgeois conservative culture. No matter how many attempts there have been to change that perspective, even to enter the building requires an act of educated choice. The Barbican is even worse, requiring a guide dog, a degree in orienteering and an IQ of about one hundred and fifty.

The terrifying part is that however physically brutal the scene on stage, the rape in *The Romans in Britain* is nothing compared with the current rape of our minds, the cultural brutalism, the mindless dumbed down reality, DIY, property, cooking, clothes, sex and talent shows that are now rampant. Unfortunately, the loophole in the law that nearly got me has not been closed and remains there as both a deterrent and a warning to those in our society who would, in the eyes of the establishment, transgress the bounds of conventional decency.

Perversely, the protests did not succeed in preventing audiences from seeing the play. Perversely, all performances were immediately sold out. What the protests did achieve, however, was to focus the audience's attention on the play's overt sexuality and, in this way, deflected debate away from the political potency of the themes. Arguably one of the most important plays of that period, *The Romans in Britain* has only twice been performed professionally since, thirty years later. An attempt was made soon after the trial by the students of Swansea University to stage the play but was thwarted by the University's legal advisers, afraid of the consequences.. The two professional productions have been in the small East London space of the Half Moon Theatre and in

2008 at the Sheffield Crucible under Sam West's tenure. I saw the production – remaining curiously detached from the experience: and yes, the attempted rape *was* staged semi clothed behind a large tree stump.

Thirty years later, in many respects censorship has got better but it appalls me that the media attitude is still as prurient as ever. It's not just the coverage of things like John Major and Edwina Curry and Sven Goran Erikson and Ulrika Johnson, Hugh Grant, Diana, Harry, Kate and Pippa – censorship now is often the result of pressure from vociferous minorities. The musical *Jerry Springer* and the Sikh play *Bechte* are both recent examples of attempts by fundamentalism to silence freedom of speech, and in the case of *Bechte* the fundamentalists succeeded, temporarily closing the Birmingham Repertory Theatre. Over eighty people walked out one night of the RSC's production of *The Marat Sade* in 2011. What did they think they were going to see forfucksake? A girl sitting next to me who had flown all the way from America to see the production on the basis of the excitable critics shrugged and said – 'I belong to a small theatre group in Wisconsin. We do worse things on stage every night.'

Mary Whitehouse may be gone, but todays' moral guardians of the nation's conscience are the self-appointed media commentators, little Englanders and Gove's Victorian gun-slingers. We constantly duck the real and important issues, failing to distinguish between the seriousness of widespread abuse by the Church and State institutions for young and old, and the grubby, groping schoolboy stupidity of various politicians and celebrities. It's as if we are still locked in the world of a Victorian peep-show. We look through the glass and snigger at the antics of the participants, and then condemn them. Our media is the most salacious and titilating in the world – and that's without phone hacking – and yet we claim the hypocritical moral high ground every time someone strays from a rigid puritanical path. I don't care if a male President or a

Prime Minister is caught with his pants down at the back of the tent as long as he doesn't lead us into war, and dispenses justice and equality along with his seed.

16

And then there's PC

If I do have a problem with freedom of speech it is that of equating Freedom of Speech with Political Correctness. At what point does PC end and censorship begin – self-imposed or other-wise? Unfair to women? Unfair to alcoholics, gays, dwarves, dogs, Blackpool landladies, Italian chefs, Lithuanian oil riggers – where do you stop? Should an anti-lesbian play be seen? Or one extolling the virtues of Fascism in concert with the 'all wogs are wankers and black bastards' brigade? Can a play propounding these views be a good play? As Irving Wardle once put it – 'the average liberal critic, confronted with a one-legged, deaf, black, lesbian, Marxist Macbeth, who had done six months for shop lifting, would find it hard to say that the Thane was not up to the role'.

When something incites it is offensive, when it satirises, it is not. If the intention is to alienate, rather than to invite understanding, then it is propaganda. But the problem with this definition is that almost anything that purports to be of an educational nature falls into the category of propaganda. It is the continual cry of the right that lefties are influencing and undermining our children. This ignores the dominant cultural thrust of our undemocratic society that ensures that our children receive a constant undiluted diet of right wing bias. The odd soft pink trickle that does filter down through the blue rinse is hardly a counter action to the mass of media-inspired brain damage that the average child undergoes most moments of his or her waking life.

So – to proselytise or not to proselytise? I want to be able to make jokes about Afghans, Jews, cripples and dyslexics; I don't want to be painted into a corner where I can't begin 'there was an Englishman, a Scotsman and an Irishman . . .' without bringing down a torrent of abuse on my head – 'what's wrong with the Welsh then?'. Humour is human behaviour. Ditto theatre. 'Nothing is either good or bad but thinking makes it so.'

Probably no other play in the entire Shakespeare canon has aroused such divergent opinions and passions in the past twenty years than *The Taming of the Shrew*. For many it is a barbaric document, dedicated to male domination and brutality, a perfect example of Shakespeare the conservative, the upholder of order, the believer in the status quo, the Elizabethan equivalent of a market force. The Thatcherite/Cameron argument.

Michael Billington in *The Guardian* once wrote – 'There is a larger question at stake than the merits or otherwise of this particular production. It is whether there is any reason to revive a play that seems totally offensive to our age and our society. My own feeling is that it should be put back firmly and squarely on the shelf.'

Those who only read the play as an offensive historical treatise, that should be locked up in its Elizabethan cupboard, are in themselves contributing to a species of conservatism that is, in itself, the obverse side of the same coin. A particular kind of old-fashioned new historicism. Shakespeare cannot be, at one and the same time, a humanist and a fascist, the two ideologies are incompatible. To forbid literature of any kind is the sharp end of censorship. The banning (not to mention the burning) of books and the shutting out of debate is perilously close to a kind of despotic totalitarianism and those who would invoke such measures would be the first to protest, throwing up their hands in horror at the mere suggestion that they were reactionary. 'But we are feminists' they cry. 'Egalitarians.'

And then there's PC

Well, egad – you could have fooled me, because a reading of the other plays, never mind the Shrew itself, makes it abundantly clear to even the most hardened misogynist that Shakespeare carried not just a torch for women's rights, but lit a bloody big bonfire. No play of course is written outside the social context that conditions the behaviour of its characters, however, *The Taming of The Shrew* cannot, in 2013, be looked on as a domestic marital comedy with an erring wife rightly and meekly submitting to the will of her husband, couched in cavorting fun, à la Burton and Taylor film. It must be analysed as the ruthless subduing of a woman by a man in a violent excess of male savagery, couched in the form of a class wish-fulfilment dream of revenge.

Katherina is a shrew. There is no use trying to pretend or act her otherwise. She breaks lutes over heads, throws pots, screams, fights, slams doors. You cannot play her sympathetically, as I have seen on a number of occasions, as a poor little misunderstood waif who won't hurt a fly. I have even seen productions where Bianca has been more fiery than Kate, a case of an actor filling a vacuum. No, the interesting point is why Katherina behaves as she does. Hers is a frustrated attempt to assert individual female values in a world of male dominated power, where the woman has no rights at all and is bartered to the highest bidder. Kate's attempt to establish independence challenges the regime and the preconceived ideas of a woman's role in society. Does Shakespeare really believe that this is the way that society should behave or is he asking for an egalitarian society of equal rights and opportunity? I believe the latter.

I had been re-reading Terry Eagleton's essay on *Macbeth*. 'The witches are the heroines of the piece . . . It is they who expose a reverence for hierarchical social order for what it is, as the pious, self-deception of a society based on routine oppression and incessant warfare. The witches are exiles from the order, inhabiting their own sisterly community on its shadowy borderlands . . .

[they] figure as the 'unconscious' of the drama, that which must be exiled and repressed as dangerous, but which is always likely to return with a vengeance . . . The witches strike at the stable, social, sexual and linguistic forms which the society of the play needs in order to survive. . . . As the most fertile force in the play, the witches inhabit an anarchic, richly ambiguous zone, both in and out of official society. They are poets, prophetesses and devotees of female cult, radical separatists who scorn male power and lay bare the hollow sound and fury at its heart. Their words and bodies mock rigorous boundaries and make sport of fixed positions, un-hinging received meanings, as they dance, dissolve and materialise.'

In October 1991 Sally Homer, my Press Officer at the ESC, faxed to me in Hamburg a copy of 'Three Witches Bearing a New Year's Greeting', a drawing by the artist Hans Baldung Grien circa 1514. The perfect poster for *Macbeth*. The original was in a gallery in Vienna and a call elicited the permission to reproduce the drawing. We used the drawing on all our publicity and programme material and distributed the poster. Coventry British Rail refused to accept it. It was 'obscene' under the definition of the British Rail Code of Acceptance of Advertisements Clause 3, whereby they could refuse to accept posters that 'depict or refer to indecency, obscenity, nudity or striptease'. (Clause 11 also prohibits ads for contraceptives – a big leap forward in the fight against AIDS and sexually transmitted diseases.) In Southampton the local newspaper wrote a leader entitled 'Knickers to Art'. Schools withdrew their booking. In Newcastle the Metro underground banned the poster, although *The Journal* newspaper wrote an article, pointing out the far more offensive and titillating way that women are used to exploit the selling of goods, irrespective of the product – from pencil sharpeners to showers and from potatoes to Porsches.

But it was the London underground that proved to be the big

cruncher. It was banned again with the lame excuse that it would inspire graffiti. We had toured internationally with *Macbeth* and this was the first occasion what we had encountered censorship of any kind. (c.f. The Poster for the film 'Disclosure'). It offered further proof, if any were needed, that London, far from being a cosmopolitan centre can be, in fact, at the level at which ideology is made, a very bourgeois city. Copulating Greek artefacts, two thousand five hundred years old, carry a content warning. Anything that drastically challenges the Establishment's right to rule is kept firmly in its place; there is a jar on the shelf labelled alternative culture and the lid is kept firmly screwed on. (Although breakthroughs in the world of art via such artists as Tracy Emmin would seem to refute this theory. But it's rather like saying that because Margaret Thatcher became Prime Minister and a woman has been on the throne for sixty years there is equal opportunity.)

The Times printed the poster on its front page – it was deemed suitable for thousands of its readers (the middle-upper class can take it, you see, they know how to discriminate) but not for *hoi poloi* who travel by tube. Calls by Mark Fisher, Shadow Minister for the Arts, and the National Campaign for the Arts to LTA, to reverse the decision were to no avail. What would they have made of the poster for Peter Zadek's *Lulu* I wonder (a bearded man on his knees, his nose buried in the pubes and labia of a naked Susa Lothar)? This refusal to display what was essentially a piece of classical art, pinpoints a struggle that the English have with their double standard, Puritanical conscience.

I received a stinker of a letter from a Catholic school teacher who brought a party of to a performance of *Romeo and Juliet* in Cardiff in 2008. They objected to Mercutio 'masturbating a champagne bottle' in the 'quivering thigh' speech. I had taken out the so-called 'dirty bits' for the schools' performances in the afternoon but this group came to the evening perf. Out of school hours. This is her letter.

'I wish to complain and express my deep dissatisfaction with regard to the standard of the evening performance of *Romeo & Juliet* on Tuesday 14th October. I attended with 11 students and a member of staff.

I was both shocked and appalled by the poor standard of the performance. One scene in particular, involving sexual acts with a Champagne bottle, disgusted everyone in our party and I feel that the direction in this scene was totally unnecessary for *Romeo & Juliet*.

Taking the reactions of all into account along with my own views to the first half of the performance I felt it necessary to make the decision to leave your theatre at the interval; this is something I have never had to do before.

As a Catholic school we follow Catholic teachings and feel that some sort of warning should have been issued with regard to the sexual content of this play; performances are chosen very carefully so as not to offend the students and their families.

As a school I have arranged many trips to see your shows, and the standards are usually very high with all who attend enjoying and getting a great deal from their visit, but we feel totally let down by your performance of *Romeo and Juliet*.

Yours sincerely,'

This was my reply.

'Re: Romeo and Juliet

I was very upset to receive your letter of complaint via the New Theatre and can only apologise for any distress caused. I take great care and pride in my Shakespeare work and am renowned for making the plays accessible and understandable for young people without compromising either the content or the quality of the work. Others have found the production extremely stimulating as you will see from the enclosed reviews.

In defence of the current production of *Romeo and Juliet* I have tried to be true to the spirit of the bawdiness of Mercutio's language in my staging of the scene in question. In a brilliant piece of juxtaposition Shakespeare has Mercutio bawling obscenities into the night, in the crudest of language, followed immediately by one of the most beautiful and lyrical of scenes in the whole canon. I have tried to highlight that juxtaposition. We have prepared a comprehensive education pack, which I would be happy to send you, with a personal essay taken from my book, 'Shakespeare the Director's Cut' Volume 1, that outlines what I believe was Shakespeare's intention.

I must point out that you brought your students to an adult performance at 7.30 in the evening, out of school hours. I do not believe in censorship of any kind; however, had you attended one of our schools' matinees, performed in school hours, you would have found the offending incident removed, as I am sensitive to the issues involved with regard to students, teachers and parents.'

It pains me that I have to what is in effect Bowdlerise Shakespeare for students of fourteen–eighteen years, most of whom are one hundred times more knowledgeable than I was at their age. No longer top-shelf but centre-stage, explicit magazines are readily available, as are the nudes in daily circulation in our tabloids: porn on the internet has moved into the mainstream and films that are explicit sometimes receive no more than a 15 rating. Fifty Shades, Chic Lit., bonkbusters, Heat, Shag, Cum – it's all there and readily available. But, in the eyes of the establishment, Art and live theatre carry with them the threat of subversion, moral and political, and the rules governing the control of their activities are muddled and open to constant abuse through misinterpretation.

Beware the politician, national or local, who preaches family values. He is usually having an affair with an 'unemployed actress' (hints of Nell Gwynn, aroma of sleaze and slut) and dressed in crutchless panties and football shirt. But he's dangerous. He can cut your subsidy. He will also attack any painting, sculpture, concert, play that deals with gay rights, sexual politics, racism etc., as 'a waste of tax payers money'. On the same day that Newcastle

City Council announced that it would cut its entire Arts budget, the Mayor of Luneburg, a town thirty miles South of Hamburg, announced in the press that he would rather see pot-holes in the road than cut the arts.

A local councillor in South Wales recently attempted to shut down a small Arts centre, employing lies, damned lies and statistics – 'we don't want a load of people practising their minority indulgent fantasies in this space', he said. When the arts are under attack from attention-seeking politicians in this fashion, it always grabs space and headlines in local newspapers and radio and TV stations. Therefore, because editors give these utterances priority and space, the arts are constantly undermined and public perception of the arts is negatively coloured. No matter how many letters are written in refutation – 'Councillor Bloggs has got his facts wrong, last year 25,000 used the arts centre, not 500', it is impossible to combat the underlying philistinism. Thus the Conservatives use statistics to decimate the benefit system. Refutation as reaction always comes off second best.

The demise of the Zahir Hadid's Cardiff Bay Opera House can be attributed in part to the hostile reaction and campaign of the media, particularly *The Western Mail* which gave Wales and the rest of the world the impression that the project was elitist, unloved, unwanted. A number of unscrupulous politicians jumped on this populist bandwagon and it was sunk. . . . Vox pops are sometimes akin to holding a referendum on hanging. Cardiff got a one hundred million pound Rugby Stadium instead. (Magnificent I hasten to add).

The plans for Hadid's opera house were replaced by something termed a 'Music Centre', until someone pointed out that this was an old fashioned term for a stereo system. To prove its proletarian credentials the new design was launched from Harry Ramsden's fish and chip emporium while guests and press stood round eating chips in newspaper. I know – I was there. To further underline its non-elitist appeal the building was to house one hundred and fifty beds in dormitories for regular visits of the Urdd – the Welsh Language National Youth organisation. So a unique design by possibly the world's leading architect morphed, through abject philistinism, into a cross between a concert hall and a Youth Hostel.

Beware self-censorship, the politics of fear. As artists we should always protest *en masse*, yet somehow we don't seem to manage to get ourselves together. We fragment, and only in sporadic outbursts do isolated groups attempt to institute change. A left-wing think tank that was formed a few years back in England, comprised of artists of the calibre of Harold Pinter and John Mortimer, was laughed at and ridiculed in the press. In other countries, no-one would dream of not taking seriously a group of intellectuals collectively aiming to supply a blue-print for the political, philosophical and artistic health of the nation. In France, such movements are the dynamo that drives their society, in ours they are laughed at.

Challenge and debate are an essential and healthy part of society. Unless we are able to challenge and challenge freely what is happening around us, then we cannot begin to express ourselves through our culture in any real sense. This is the lid of the social pressure cooker that the establishment has tried all the time to force down. I would like to think that it is becoming increasingly more difficult to keep that lid down, but it amazes me that we submit passively to ministerial pressure, and are crushed by the forces of a juggernaut steamrolling government, thus allowing our civil liberties to become ever more eroded and restricted. (See Tony Blair's *Freedom of Information Bill*, the Posh Boys attempt to withdraw the right to Trial by Jury, the *Bill of Human Rights*, withdrawal of Legal Aid etc.) What we are witnessing in the first decades of the 21st century is a frightening process of 'normalisation'.

Which brings me to a tribute to one of the great PC boundary-crossers of the last fifty years – Jerome Savary who died in March 2013. Jerome was the founder of one of the great seminal companies of the 60s and 70s, Le Grand Magic Circus. He became Artistic Director of the TNP – Le Theatre National Populaire de Chaillot, and later the Opera Comique, exciting French and foreign audiences alike with his anarchic extravaganzas.

Jerome was a larger than life *bon viveur* with a heart the size of a hot air balloon. Early in 2000 he bought a whole village in the South of France and handed it over to those performers from Le Grand Magic Circus who had fallen on hard times, to live and work there. The lithe, svelte figure of the Cabotin from the Circus days gave way latterly to a girth of Falstaffian proportions and an appetite for good living to match, which he shared generously with the world. I know, for I was on the receiving end on a number of occasions in Paris and Hamburg. He used to get so homesick for Paris that he would literally commute daily by plane from cities around Europe, going back home every night.

One day he flew in to Hamburg at 9.30 a.m., started a rehearsal in the Schauspielhaus at 10 oclock and at 11.00 called a coffee break. The cast trooped down to the canteen and waited for the call back.

And waited. And waited.

At 12.30 somebody decided to find out what was happening. A couple of hours away from Paris was all that Jerome could manage. He'd flown back again.

He rang me up once (imagine Poirot crossed with 'Allo Allo') 'Michel – zey 'ave asked me to do my production of ze *Bourgeois Gentilhomme* at ze National Theatre in Londres. 'Ow much will zey pay me?'

'Well, the most a director gets is about £8,000 tops, but because it's you I'm sure they'd give you ten.'

'Ten zousand pounds?! (Horrified). Zat would not keep me in lobsters!'

And he didn't do it.

And then there's PC

He did however come over to do the musical *Metropolis*. He invited me to come and watch a chunk of the technical rehearsal. I wandered in to the auditorium and there on stage was a familiar figure in a blue belted overcoat and a red scarf. He was shouting. 'You waste my time, you waste my time! You know what it costs to pay me per minute? I am expensive. I am the second most expensive director in Europe after Zefarelli!'

He rang me up ruefully. 'Michel, zey have banned me from ze theatre'. For the whole of the production week before the show opened bouncers were stationed at the doors of the Piccadilly Theatre with orders not to let in a rotund Frenchman in a blue overcoat and a red scarf.

A wild, irrepressible showman, with his goats, sheep, dwarves, donkeys, horses and chickens he belonged to an era of theatre when anything was possible on stage, before Animal Rights, Health and Safety and Political Correctness took over our lives, forbidding actors to climb higher than two metres unless attached to a wire. I loved him.

17

Heavy Bag Acting

'Who would fardels bear? To sweat and groan under the
strain of a weary life?'

(*Hamlet*)

I was watching two actors on the stage of the Greek National
Theatre in Athens struggling with a huge sack, obviously filled
with feathers, polystyrene and scrunched up old tissue paper. They
were doing heavy-bag acting. It's an off-shoot of old-man-with-
walking-stick, drunk-with-bottle, three-course-meal-in-thirty-
seconds, heavy-boob acting (the outstretched palms bobbing up
and down as if weighing two water-melons).

The problem with this kind of naturalism is that most of the
time it is not even true to its own convention. I have no problem
with essence-of-old-woman or essence-of-heavy-metal. What irks
is if, when the true intention is to make me believe that a person
is really old or an object is really heavy, the attempt to demonstrate
these qualities founders on the rock of bad acting. That is not to
say that I want ultimate reality on stage, illusion and suspension
of disbelief are the bedrock of all theatre, but if someone is
working a real sewing machine or someone is drinking from a
real pot with real coffee and sugar, then at least I had the right to
expect in the Greek production that, if the acting was not up to
it, the sack the two actors were carrying contained a couple of
lead weights in it to prevent the two clowns looking like Mike

and Bernie rejects. In this instance, to convince, the illusion of the sack being heavy and the reality had to coincide.

One knows that this sloppiness will often extend to all aspects of a production. In the case of the Greek performance, a play about a feuding, peasant, mountain family, the actors were all palpably middle-class in their mannerisms and in their dress, a frequent problem of the English stage, even in an age of supposed equal accent. (Spare me genteel forays into darkest Millwall – Osborne dropping his aitches to empathise with the employees in Morrisons. And I was singularly unconvinced by a series of clean-cut posh boys playing French working class revolutionaries in the film of *Les Miserables*).

I don't mind if what is presented is a parable of some form, a heightened view of a community where the historical and geographical particular engenders a universal and where the emotions and subtext are more important than the naturalistic detail, but please, not masquerading as a slice of life. Nevertheless, the naturalistic theatre has conducted a never ending search for the fourth wall which has led it into a whole series of absurdities. For ultimate reality the stage can never match film and TV which have made naturalism their natural home. It is difficult to assess the possible damage that Stanislavski has done in the last hundred years to our expectations of the theatre, but there is no doubt that, despite the theories and work of a number of theatre revolutionaries, no-one has been able to check the process by which theatre as an art form has grown increasingly personal and individual in both its language and its vision. This process which began to concern artists in every field in the first third of the 20th century has continued after the interruption of World War II with even greater and more widespread vigour in Britain since the stage revolution of 'kitchen sink' drama in the 50s. TV and film have contributed massively to the disintegration, but why the stage had to follow so abjectly in their wake is a mystery. Illusion, illusion,

illusion. It is as if Artaud, Mayerholt, Piscator, Brecht, Grotowski etc., have all passed us by. I'm as guilty as anyone, having strived to achieve cinematic reality for forty years with a series of contemporary Shakespeare productions.

Observe elderly people. Their rhythm. Their pace – or lack of it. Feet, hands. For a young actor to capture the essence of age something as simple as the slowness with which all tasks are accomplished can create the illusion; or the solitariness, the insularity of a life lived and burning itself inexorably to ash, determined by an inner stillness, a sadness. It is only important to decide first of all whether the aged person is a sprightly eighty or a broken sixty (or vice versa). If an old man uses a stick, it could be for a variety of reasons.

Let us say he has a bad leg, his left one. (As a gout sufferer my identification is complete). He cannot put weight on the leg, he leans on his stick, held in the right hand which moves forward in conjunction with the left leg and takes the weight, leaning to the right instead of the weight being taken on the left leg. A somewhat boring explanation, I grant, but how often does one see this lack of any apparent handicap in performance. It's akin to watching Tony Sher play Richard III at the RSC, palpably a superbly fit physical actor doing circus stunts on a couple of crutches, not a sniff of an affliction in sight. For all his mannerisms, Olivier wouldn't have made that mistake and would still have wrung all the physical possibilities out of the situation.

Hitoshi Takagi was seventy when he played Sorin for me in *The Seagull* in Tokyo. He would cycle to rehearsals and do the warm-up energetically with the rest of the actors. When we came to rehearse he adopted a bent-double stance, a quavering voice and a shaky hand, that trembled as he lent on his stick, the other hand holding his side. Joke old man acting.

'Why are you doing that?'

'Sorin is old.'

'How old?'

'Sixty.'

'How old are you?'

'Seventy.'

'But you don't behave like that?'

'Ah. I'm different.'

All people are different, particularly old ones, they've had more time to work at it.

Chekov once attended rehearsals of *The Seagull* at the Moscow Arts Theatre and one of the actors told him that off-stage there would be frogs croaking, dragon-flies humming and dogs barking.

'Why' asked Chekov.

'Because it's realistic' replied the actor.

'Realistic?' Chekov laughed. Then after a short pause he said

'The stage is art. There is a series of paintings by Kramskoy in which the faces are portrayed superbly. What would happen if you cut the nose out of one of the paintings and substituted a real one? The nose would be 'realistic' but the picture would be ruined.'

One of the actors proudly told Chekov that the director intended to bring the entire household including a woman with a child crying on stage at the close of the third act. Chekov said 'He mustn't. It would be like playing *pianissimo* on the piano and having the lid suddenly crash down.'

'But in life it often happens that the *pianissimo* is interrupted quite unexpectedly by the *forte*', said one of the actors.

'Yes, but the stage demands a degree of artifice' said Chekov. 'There is no fourth wall. Besides the stage is art, it reflects the quintessence of life and there is no need to introduce anything superfluous on it.'

I was in Washington D.C. directing *The Mayor of Zalamea* when Michael Rudman's production of *Death of a Salesman* with Dustin Hoffman in the lead arrived into town at the Kennedy Centre. Michael and I were Associates together at the National for eight years. A tall rangy Texan from Austin who got carved up pretty badly by Felicity Kendal. He lost her for many years to Tom Stoppard. Michael is a very funny man. He used to make me laugh. He would attend a preview of my productions and come up with bizarre suggestions for improvements. 'Hey, you know what would make the production work? Reverse the Acts – play Part 2 first.'

I called Michael up at the Watergate Hotel where he was staying. A furtive, haunted voice answered the phone, dripping with suspicion.

'Hello?'

'This is Michael Bogdanov.'

'Mike, for Christ sake, get over here as fast as you can.'

The phone slammed down. 'Puzzled' is the word I would use to describe my reaction. A haggard, unshaven face peered round the door in response to my knock, eyes bloodshot, hair lank and greasy. A hand shot out and dragged me in, slamming the door shut behind. The room looked like it was under siege. Dirty plates, half-eaten take-aways, bottles and old socks decorously encircled a Mount Vesuvius of cigarette cartons and ash that formed a centre piece to Suite 114.

'It's good to see you, I haven't been out for a week.'

It transpired that everything with the production had been going swimmingly until Philadelphia and then, after a batch of bad reviews, Hoffman had turned against Rudman, encouraging the rest of the cast to do the same. He was re-directing scenes himself and would not speak to Michael, whose only means of communication, after sneaking in at the back of the theatre to view performances, was to pass notes on to the actors via Arthur Miller. I persuaded Michael to come out and have something to eat. He dressed in scarf, overcoat and dark glasses, although it was a bitterly cold February, frightened of meeting Hoffman.

We did just that.

The lift descended to the foyer, opened, and there he was. Michael scuttled back in like a startled rabbit and we shot back up again to the 10th floor. After a decent interval, we finally made it to an eaterie in Georgetown.

'What's Hoffman like in the part?'

'Wait till you see him and then tell me.'

We sneaked in at the back of the auditorium. And then he came on stage. Dustin Hoffman as Willie Loman. Almost bent double, neck craning forward like a constipated goose, eyes bulging, feet flicking out – toe, heel, toe, heel – arms stiff as ramrods, two feather-light suitcases on the end of them.

Heavy-bag acting.

We left. The production got raves in Washington. Michael was the toast of the town. They were all speaking to him again. The bastards.

18

Middle-Distance Gazing

Tim Burton ruined a great little musical in *Sweeney Todd*. Johnny Depp is unbelievably one-dimensional. No evidence at all of Depp's skill as a barber. The best in London? I wouldn't touch him with a barber's pole let alone go for a shave. And it's not even his voice singing said the credits. The amount of blood was rivalled only by Peter O'Toole emerging on stage at the Old Vic from what looked like a bath-tub of ketchup in Bryan Forbes' production of *Macbeth*. 'A little water clears us of this deed . . . ' The audience cheered like the Kop. I know. I was there.

Helena Bonham Carter is hopelessly miscast as Mrs. Lovett. Consummate in the right parts – *The King's Speech* – why does Ms B.C. keep being cast in Dick Van Dykian mockney roles? I once turned her down for Perdita in *The Winter's Tale*. But then I once turned down Joe Fiennes for Romeo – for reasons other than acting I hasten to add. He was still at RADA and the rehearsal schedule would have been horrendous. And in 2006 I sacked Katherine Jenkins – from the UK Holocaust Memorial Event at the Wales Millennium Centre. Katherine was born a couple of doors down from my mother's house in Neath. Normally we Welsh are soldered together but for two months Katherine had messed me around – or she and her agent had – and then she announced the night before the event, after we'd spent £500 that day specially transposing the whole orchestral score for her, that

174

she was unable to sing the solo from Tippett's *A Child of Our Time*. Could she sing something from her album instead – Amazing Grace perhaps?. Fuck off.

'Who's topping the bill?', asked Katherine's idiot agent, when I told him.

(This is the UK Holocaust Memorial Event remember.)

'The Queen, Prince Philip, Tony Blair, General Dallaire . . .'

Silence. 'Oh. I suppose they're not getting paid then . . .'

* * *

I digress. The point of this story is that Depp was doing 'for fifteen years all I've ever wanted to do is slit throats and that's why I stare all the time unblinking into the middle distance' acting. 'To be or not to be', eyes fixed on the 'Exit' sign at the back of the circle. 'Oh my orchard! My beautiful orchard!', the cherry trees apparently 150 ft high, their tops somewhere around Row 5 of the Gallery.

Forty-five degree acting. Middle-distance gazing. It denotes contemplation, mystery, unfathomable depths. The woman has a soul full of sadness, the man has a problem of some sort. 'Oh, if you could only understand me!'

It would be easy to excuse this exercise in non-communication as 'including all the house' if it were not so commonplace a substitute for real emotion. Middle-distance gazing becomes an attempt to impress on the audience the reality of the feeling, eyes misting over, fixed unseeingly on some distant point, the soul mirrored in the slight flicker of pain that twitches the cheek. All that the people in the front row see is the double chin or the angular lump of the Adam's apple. Not a lot of sentiment there.

Soliloquies are the danger point. Thinking out loud is denoted by the head jerking heavenwards and the hands (if male) thrust deep in the pockets (if female) reaching out to unscrew some distant light-bulb, the other hand catching at the throat to

175

dislodge an errant fishbone. It is one more hangover from our more melodramatic Victorian forbears. Michael MacLiammoir, the Shakespearean doyen of the Irish stage, was the light-bulb screwer *par excellence*. He would elongate himself on the floor, one leg curled under him, one hand supporting himself, the other reaching out in supplication in the direction of the 60 watt, fingers slightly spread, hollowed and revolving 'Oh for a muse of fire . . .', screw, screw, screw.

People in repose, thinking, mostly have their eyes cast down. Retreat into oneself, the body assumes a modesty, a stillness. This then is the 'soliloquy contemplative' mode. Stanislavski style. On the other hand, soliloquies are not necessarily to oneself: they are, or were, a convention for sharing thoughts with an audience. True, there are people in the circle, the gallery. But there are also people in the front row, Row F, Seat 104. They need to share as well.

And expect responses. Ask the right questions and you get the wrong answers. 'Is this a dagger that I see before me?' 'Who calls me villain?' 'He who knows better how to tame a shrew now let him speak'. There would surely have been debate in the Elizabethan theatre at such moments. Question and answer sessions are now consigned to pantomime and stand-up and considered infantile.

On the other hand, if you're talking to a person, how often do you stand looking over their shoulder, anxiously scanning the sky for the seagull? Or in the middle of a tense moment with a loved one, turn away, eyes skywards –

'For God's sake, John, why won't you look at me!'

'I can't Melanie, my neck has locked back on my shoulders and my eyeballs are glued somewhere around the middle of the cornice piece.'

'Tell me about it, Bill.'

'It all began one evening on stage, when I had this compulsive urge to look at the chandelier in the auditorium. Now I find I can't stop myself – please help me Melanie.'

Middle-Distance Gazing

'Poor love, I think you need a course of middle distance gazing therapy.'

'What's that, Melanie?'

'Basically, it's a mixture of Artaud and Piscator, with a dash of Michael Chekov and a touch of Brook Bond.'

Depp had it all in spades. And as for the geography of the building . . . that chute would have landed slap bang in the middle of a tray of Bonham Lovett's pies.

19

German *Kunst*

Since the year 2000 I have been working pretty constantly in Germany, give or take back in Wales – more specifically Hamburg, where I now live with my German wife and children. In contrast to the high Blockbuster classics and musicals with casts of thousands that were my lot in the previous forty years or so, I have been directing, with one or two exceptions, in small theatres and with small casts – new plays, the latest British and American work, the world premiere of a new version of *Mephisto* by Helen Edmundson. Successfully I might add modestly, having won four or five awards during that time. I mention the fact not out of pride but because in Britain – specifically London – out of sight out of mind. To fight director, Malcolm Ranson – 'Bogdanov? is he still around?' On being introduced to the current Musical Director at the Globe Theatre – 'Michael Bogdanov? Didn't you used to direct?' I did and do. Often ridiculously prolifically.

As I write this on May 1st it's a national holiday in Germany as it is all over Europe. Except the UK. We're the only country that celebrates May 1st on May 2nd, 3rd, 4th, 5th, 6th – depending on the first Monday in the month and we call it a Bank Holiday. Why the banks should play such a dominating role in determining our leisure time is just another example, not of a secular society, but one dominated by capital. Bank employees are so overworked, poor things, that they need a day off.

I once arranged a cricket match in Hamburg between the

178

National Theatre in London and a team that I assembled from the Schauspielhaus and other Brits in Hamburg. I'm Honorary President of the RNT, having founded the club with three others in 1981. The match was a huge success. We took over the pitch from the Hamburg Polo Club and the seventy-five year old groundsman there rolled a wicket and marked it up. He was very proud of the fact he had learnt how to do it from British airmen in 1947, who used to play matches there regularly, and knew about yards, popping creases, and boundaries. The team, led by John Langley, had a terrific time and we planned it again for the following year, 1991, for the Whitsun week-end. John organised the flights and I booked the pitch, arranged the hotels and catering, and the week before called John to finalise the schedule.

'See you next week-end', I said.

'What?'

'See you next week-end.'

'You mean in three weeks-time.'

'No – next week-end, Whitsun.'

'That's May 28th', he said.

The penny dropped. I had been working on the Whitsun, the religious festival determined like Eatser by the calendar, the rest of the world acknowledges. John had always meant the end of May Bank Holiday. The poll pitch wasn't available and there was no alternative: hotels were full. We had to cancel flights, hotels, and call the whole thing off. *Vive la revolution*.

In 2010 I did an interview for NDR radio about my production of *Elling*, an adaptation of the Norwegian, Oscar nominated film, at the Hamburger Kammerspiele. The lady suggested that the play was a bit 'Klaumock' – a derogatory word for a kind of trousers-down theatre that the German literary elite despise. I nearly got very angry. It took me back twenty years to the Schauspielhaus and the criticism by the Kunst brigade that I only ever produced *Unterhaltungstheater* – entertainment.

Laughter, in the tortured minds of many German critics, is *verboten*. Life and art are serious matters and frivolous Welsh directors should be run out of town. Well, I broke the box office and audience numbers two years running in Germany's largest National Theatre – one thousand three hundred and fifty seats – a feat that in the twenty years since nobody has come near equalling. And anybody who thinks that steel-workers, ship-builders, cleaners, sweepers and bus-drivers flock to the National Theatre to see 'Klaumok' productions of *Hamlet*, *The Tempest*, *Maria Stuart* etc., needs a brain transplant.

I am probably in something of a foreign minority in believing that the Germans have a good sense of humour. Even the German themselves laugh at their reputation: (Question: 'What's the Shortest book in the world?' Answer: '1001 Years of German Humour'). Certainly my experience of directing comedy there has never given me grounds to think otherwise, having had to make no concessions whatsoever to culturally comic differences. The German people laugh at the same things, enjoy the same verbal gymnastics, jokes, puns, stage business as any other audience. The problems only begin for Teutonic comic consciousness when the subject moves to 'life' and 'art'. Humour for them plays no part in life or art, humour at that point equates to frivolity, lack of seriousness, 'oberflächlichkeit' – superficiality. Life and art for the Germans are inseparable and humour belongs to neither.

Herein lies a fundamental difference between the German and the Anglo-Saxon attitude – so near and yet so far. For the funning and the punning British, life and art have absolutely nothing whatsoever to do with each other, but humour is an essential part of both. By the cut of his comic capers so shall ye know what class of a person he is (or she).

This locking of linguistic antlers is part of a macho and particularly male British characteristic where each protagonist seeks, as quickly as possible, to occupy the humorous high-ground, thereby gaining an instant advantage through probing for an opponent's cultural weak spots, identifying their origins, pigeon-holing, buttoning, nailing. No comparable cut and thrust exists in a Germanic encounter, class and origins for the most part being of no interest, the attempt at building a post-war democracy patently more successful than that of their British brethren. Mind you, any nation that for many years had as its Chancellor, Kohl, a man whose name in translation means 'cabbage' (or 'money' in slang – highly appropriate in the circumstances), was asking for trouble from the British tabloids. As a demonstration of what he thought of current German Politik, Kunst and Kohl, Frank Castorf – *wunderkind* of the rejuvenated Volksbuehne Theater in old East Berlin (all seats five marks – bring your sleeping bag and dog) in his production of Goethe's *Stella* had an actor smash a cabbage (Kohl) over a bust of Goethe, stick a bratwurst in his mouth and then urinate all over him. Well, I thought it was funny – at the time – though it doesn't sound so rib-tickling seeing it in print.

But that is one of the joys of working in Germany – not urinating over busts of Goethe or of anyone else – but that one may do so should one so desire. On the German stage there are no hang ups – political, sexual or any other-al; everything and anything goes in the relentless quest for truth in what is seen as an essentially 'moralisches'- moral – theatre. I am being a bit economical with the *Wahrheit* here – many directors still have difficulties with military matters, with portraying invading armies as comprised of anything other than tortured, reluctant servers of their masters and only Peter Zadek has yet dared portray Shylock as a nasty piece of work. It's significant that *The Producers* was a flop in Berlin. Springtime for Hitler was a season too far.

This free-for-all approach breeds actors who are daring, adventurous and take the kinds of risks with language and body that can turn Pinter into a night on the Reeperbahn with a maraud-ing tiger. Of course many directors go to extremes to *épater les bourgeois*, but it is a mark of the bourgeois' lack of 'bourges' in most German cities that it refuses to be epated and insists on discussing, with straight face and eyes bright with misunderstanding, every new outrageous offering that is literally dandled and dangled in front of it.

When what is offered up in this fashion works, the results can be electrifying as with Peter Zadek's *Lulu*, a brilliant five-hour hymn to rudery, consummately portrayed by Susa Lothar, naked for almost the entire time. When it doesn't, it is shrugged off as an experiment. Indeed Frank Castorf's production of Jean Paul Satre's *Kean* which in England might have landed director and actors in jail, was voted one of the ten best productions of 2010. Nobody would dream of talking about grant withdrawal.

This emphasises one of the fundamental differences between German and, particularly, British theatre. As you would expect of a country that has had a National Theatre of sorts for two hundred and fifty years, albeit of the federal kind under Dukedoms, the belief that culture is a vital and important part of a nation's health runs deep. Accordingly in Germany artists are able to contribute politically, culturally, socially and aesthetically to the life of the country. Unlike their British counterparts, they have status. At least the Irish government appears to believe that writers are important enough national assets for them not to have to pay tax. In Britain a philistinism of some sort has always reigned, at national and local level.

No. The German system, with its one hundred and thirty-two State theatres and a network of some six hundred others totally or partially funded, is to be applauded, but the system is open to abuse and is often that untranslatable word 'bequem', 'zugellos', 'selbst-gefällig' – self-indulgent.

All this 'indulgence', is possible because the German system of Federal funding allows for it. The total spent by the City of Hamburg alone on the arts is almost as much as that for the whole of England. Amongst many other things Germany understands the basic rule that Theatre, Opera and Ballet are labour intensive and that, in order to make them available and affordable to all, subsidy must be high. Opera, left to market forces would possibly consist of half a dozen singers and a quintet. The *real* cost of subsidising The Royal Opera House in London, (there are seventy-five in Germany, two and a half in England), if you wish all seats to be priced at the equivalent of £10, would be in excess of £60 million, not £20 million. Britain has yet to catch up with the equation – (will it ever?) – that theatre/opera/ ballet equals people equals wages equals subsidy. No, let's have a lottery chaps, and tap big business for corporate hosting, that's the way to fund the arts, get these wankers off our backs. In Germany most cities would no more think of cutting their subsidy to the arts than they would think of cutting their throats.

If there is one sweeping generalisation to be made it is that the German theatre is all content (kunst) and no form and that the English is all form and no content, (form as represented by the well-made play, representational acting, functional design, rhetorical or natural delivery of the text). However, when the two things do combine in Germany, the possibility of great theatre, the kind that changes lives, is there in all its political, social and moral glory, a feeling that is often absent in Britain in the well-made telly play, the Stoppardian literary crossword-puzzle and the designer orientated musical madness, that *espèce de transatlantic* theatrical rabies that has invaded Britain without the necessity of a tunnel. (Though the recent trend away from mind-numbing compilations to tackle more interesting themes – gives cause for hope.)

Where the English presentation is often all lighting design, hydraulically challenged symmetry and the acting homely or rhetorical, the German can sometimes seem perverse to the point of absurdity. A setting will be so abstractly impressionist as to have no relationship with the text whatsoever, and the lights will point anywhere rather than at the actor. A chair brilliantly lit, 'to be or not to be' etc., intoned from somewhere at the back of the stage in stygian gloom. And one could be forgiven for thinking that the problem for the citizens in *Coriolanus* is less a question of bread deficiency and rather more the fact that the streets are thronging with the mentally challenged left-overs from *Peer Gynt*'s Egyptian nut-house. Twitching, itching, limping and frothing – obligatory tools of the Teutonic trade – would fail, I suspect, to get many votes for specialist inclusion in English drama courses.

The problem is this German obsession with Kunst – literally 'art' with a huge dollop of arty, not to mention farty, thrown in. And Kunstpolitik. The Germans are aware of the tortuous, convoluted metaphysical cartwheels that they turn on the stages of their State theatres but are incapable of doing anything about it. It is significant that the German language contains no suitable translation for the word 'self-indulgent'. Trying to explain what it means is met with stares of incomprehension. Isn't that what life is all about – the tortured exploration of self? (Unlike us who never believe any description of ourselves. Have you ever met an English person who admits to being a prude?)

The problem is an historical one. After the devastation wreaked by the Second World War, some of the first buildings to be restored and rebuilt were theatres and opera houses, the belief being that self-respect and pride could only be regained by a celebration of the better aspects of German culture, indeed, that the future moral and political health of the nation depended upon it. It speaks volumes for the differences between the two countries that in Britain people flocked in their millions to football, while in Germany it was to theatre and opera. Audiences enthusiastically embraced not only their own writers but O'Neill, Anouilh, Shaw *et al* – all the writers who hitherto had been banned, the diet complimented by a dash of world classics – in a bewildered attempt to come to grips with what had happened, through an investigation of their cultural past.

German *Kunst*

The shock and trauma ran deep and a wave of writers (many of them Swiss, one has to say) emanated from that time who articulated these complex emotions and feelings. It was left to Brecht to return from enforced exile abroad and lay the foundations of a political theatre amidst the wreckage of old Berlin. The 60s saw the triumph of art over realism, the victory of the director over the author, the bonding of the critic and the Kunstkonzept. The Berlin Wall may have come down but nearly twenty-five years later the impenetrable Kunst Wall is still in place

The consequence of this has been an almost complete absence of new plays on the Staatstheater stages. This avoidance of confronting guilt through contemporary writing has meant that any political or philosophical analysis of the problems facing the German people was confined to re-runs of plays such as 'Nathan der Weise', 'Prinz Friederich von Homburg', 'Egmont', etc., an attitude that has endured to the present day. With a crucial difference. People are no longer going in their millions to serious theatre. But imported musicals, and the occasional home-grown one, are thriving. As are the smaller Private theatres to whom falls the task of nourishing narrative theatre. And that resistance has accelerated. No one wants to see yet *another* re-run of a deconstructed 'Emilia Galotti'.

From a high point in the late sixties, audiences have gradually declined as mobility, affluence, leisure pursuits, TV and other rival attractions have taken over. Yet subsidy continued to increase on a regular and annual basis on the assumption that the community at large should still be provided for on the old basis. The result was more and more subsidy for fewer and fewer audience (my old theatre, the Schauspielhaus in Hamburg, is a good example, and Hamburg is a city where they do still go to the theatre). And, with notable exceptions, new writing is *still* absent from German stages. Instead of re-unification providing the springboard for a re-appraisal of German cultural politics, theatres have not only sounded a retreat but have positively led a stampede away from any confrontation with the present. The result is the current re-appraisal of German Arts funding. The phrase 'value for money' has even been heard. . . .

In effect, the controlling artistic influence is in the hands of a very few people. As Oxbridge dominates English cultural life, so German theatre is led by the nose by a small group of critics and editors of the cultural sections of the leading newspapers – 'Fuelleton Chefs' – comprising mainly of the magazine 'Theater Heute', the weekly 'Die Zeit' – plus the three daily newspapers, 'The Frankfurter Allgemeine', 'The Frankfurter Rundschau' and 'The Süddeutsche Zeitung'. These arbiters of public taste rule, but it's not okay. What they say today, others will write and report tomorrow. It's a game of Follow My Leader; collectively the German critics behave with as much imagination as a bunch of sheep and they pursue theatre directors with a tenacity that our tabloids reserve for fellating soap-stars, philandering royals, expense-fiddling politicians and money-laundering football managers.

Thus the favoured few keep German Kulturpolitik in thrall. Until recently they were aided and abetted in this by an ageing cartel of Intendants – Staats theatre Chief Executives – and 'star' directors. They circulate from theatre to theatre, usually taking with them their administrative, technical and artistic teams, plus their entire ensemble of actors. Is it any wonder that Vienna feels like Köln, feels like Berlin, feels like Munich used to feel before it felt like Hanover. This was known as 'the carousel', a meritocratic merry-go-round which has only recently given way to a new breed of thrusting 'young Turks'. And would that the Turkish community, which is a large one, were reflected in the mainstream of German cultural life.

But the influence of minority cultures, represented by the literally hundreds of thousands of refugees that in the space of a few years have poured over the open German borders, is hardly anywhere to be seen except in the street demonstrations against their presence. The task has been left to the many small, private theatres – a misnomer really, many are in receipt of a percentage of public subsidy but are heavily reliant on their box office income. Nevertheless it is often here that you will find the new or imported contemporary play.

Claus Peymann, Stein and other 'star' directors (the average age of the quartet running the Berliner Ensemble in the late 1990's was over sixty) are the driving force behind what is seen on German stages. And their taste is for a self-absorbed endless reconstruction of Germany's past and present guilt, through this endless recycling of old plays.

Part of this phenomenon, not accepting the challenge of new work, is fear – fear of criticism, fear of being exposed, fear of directorial failure. This can sometimes lead to the loneliness of the long distance rehearsal – Stein one year for Faust; the continual postponing of premieres – or the abandoning of projects altogether – paying off an entire artistic team engaged for that period – certain directors are famous for starting but not finishing. These overly-long rehearsal periods often lead to baffling, overly-long productions – Andrea Breth, one of the few female directors to break into what is an almost exclusively male club – a four hour *Zerbrochene Krug* (*The Broken Jug*) in Munich, a play that at most is ninety minutes straight through. The aforementioned Kean at the Volksbuehne five and a half hours. We emerged blinking into the almost dawn at 1.30 am. Where is the sense that audiences may have an hour's journey home? Or have children who get up at 6.00am for the German early school start? And the current trend in young directors is even more worrying from the playwright's point of view.

Failure to engage new voices to articulate the problems of Germany's present has led to a new breed of directorial deconstructionists. Having seemingly exhausted the possible permutations of orthodox productions of the classics, these shakers and movers, have blithely deconstructed their way to the top of the Kunst table. Of course, sometimes these pieces achieve depth, insight and a theatricality that is exhilarating. More often than not they succeed in justifying Peter Brook's definition of dead theatre, or, more prosaically, bore the arse off all and sundry. For example, Christian Marthaler (who, I hasten to add, is one of the most talented and original directors at work today) specialises in whole casts falling asleep on stage and often achieves the ultimate in audience participation by having an entire theatre joining in this somnabulistic celebration. (Those who haven't already left, that is.)

It follows that the wonderful breed of German actor is often the plaything and puppet of directors. This is particularly unfortunate for, at their best, German actors combine the physicality of the Americans or Japanese, with the psychological and textual approach of the English, making them some of the most exciting performers in the world. If by some chance (someone taking a chance) a new play does find its way onto the main stage (not a deconstructed old one), it is immediately snapped up for performance all over the German-speaking world. Nobody wants to be the first to jump but when someone does – they all jump.

Eberhardt Witt, Intendant of the Bayerische Staats-schauspielhaus, Munich from 1990–2000, once said to me shortly before retiring, – 'Why should I do new plays? I would rather do classics than a not very good piece directed not very well by a young assistant, acted not very well by inexperienced actors'. At least in Britain we do lots of small new plays, even if we can't afford to do big ones. This blocking of a proper theatrical artery, often not even being prepared to use studio theatres as a nurturing ground for young talent, leads to the oft-taken liberties at the top, directors indulging their fantasies to the full without the problem of having to help shape new writing. Those writers that are performed are now somewhat long in the tooth or gone. Tancred Dorst, Kroetz, Botto Strauss, Heiner Muller, Peter Turini, George

Tabori, Peter Handke, Ralph Hochhut. Put like that the list is formidable and gives the impression that new writing is not only alive and well but potentially bursting with health. But most of these, if they are still alive, are in their sixties, seventies, even eighties. Even the Austrian, Elfrida Jelinek, has long been acclaimed as a novelist.

The language of the German Staatstheater is formal Hoch-Deutsch. And therein lies the difficulty that local writers (such as there are) have with exploring local themes or writing about contemporary issues. The only accents that are tolerated are national – Austrian, Swiss, Bavarian (which counts as national) or German spoken with the accent of another country and therefore unavoidable – Rumanian, Polish, Russian, etc.,. It is for many directors, actors and audiences inconceivable to have the grave-diggers in *Hamlet* played with a Sächsisch or a Hessisch accent. Where we would not dream of putting a play about modern Dublin or Newcastle on stage without aspiring to *some* level of authenticity, Germany would only find that colourful language offensive.

Unlike the transformation that English acting went through in the fifties and sixties, Germany has not yet had its stage revolution. Accordingly dialect and accent are frequently missing and the local play is, therefore, almost non-existent on the main stages. Dialect and accent are only for *Volkstheater*, theatre for the masses and, therefore, banished from the high temples of Kunst. Naturalism, the staple diet of the modern theatre world-wide, is looked down on as a means of communication, both in the writing and in the acting. Surrealism, expressionism, abstraction – these are the forms that dominate. (Honourable exceptions are made for Chekov and Ibsen and possibly a few Austrians, but even they have to take their turn in the deconstruction bumper car.) If new plays from the English-speaking world are performed (the translation industry is a whole other *Fischkessel*) there is an inability to confront the narrative form head on.

Howard Brenton, on seeing an inexplicable production of his *Moscow Gold* in Berlin could exclaim – 'What on earth was that about? What have they done to my play?' And see them try to do Ayckbourn! A reputable critic, writing of *Dancing at Lugnasa* – winner of twenty-four awards in Ireland, Britain and America – can say 'what on earth has this piece to do with Germany?' Anyone who has an Abitur in English is on the translation bandwagon. New plays in English are translated even before they are performed in Britain. (Strange that they will do ours, but we won't do theirs.) This love affair with Anglo-American drama has now spread to East Germany along with the Wessie directors and, where for thirty years the dominant repertoire was Russian, Czech, Polish, etc., now it is Arthur Miller, Tennessee Williams, David Mamet and Neil Simon. One can't help feeling that East Germany has given the West many of its best directors, actors, writers, designers and given hamburgers in return.

Nevertheless, the wind of change is blowing through Germany. The closing of the Schiller Theater in Berlin a few years back, until its demise one of the world's most heavily subsidised theatres, sent a series of shock waves rolling through the German artistic community, reverberations of which have been felt in the rest of Europe. Yet in many ways it was neither unexpected nor surprising. The demise of the Berlin Wall had produced a brief period of hope that the artists in West Germany's moralistic, over-indulgent, cultural community would grasp at last the somewhat prickly political nettle of reunification and play an historic role in the shaping of the future. Cultural copulation after thirty years asunder was seen as an opportunity for Ossies and Wessies alike to inspect each others artistic navels and embrace the differences that would emerge in the aftermath of reconciliation.

Some hopes. If anything, the social, cultural and political upheaval of the last years in the Eastern *bloc* has seen theatre in the West even more of an insular, elitist occupation than it was before.

Western artists behaved like spoilt children, the Wall, their lollipop, having been taken away from them. While it was there they could always moan, groan and passionately pound the table. Without it – *nix*. No-one had thought about it not being there.

The writing is on the wall. Monstrous temples for musicals are burgeoning everywhere. Berlin is becoming culturally two cities again: on the one hand the most *outré* and vibrant counter-culture of anywhere in Europe, on the other a musical city – two about Marlene Dietrich in the space of a year, each as excruciating as the other. *Phantom, Buddy, The Lion King, Tarzan, Rocky* and *Curse of the Vampire* rule in Hamburg, *Starlight Express* still in Bochum, *Miss Saigon* in Stuttgart and Andrew Lloyd-Webber and Cameron Macintosh constructed two new monsters to house *Sunset Boulevard* and *Les Misérables*, a custom built Theatre in Bremen housed *Dr Jekyll and Mr. Hyde*, and a Berlin equivalent for *The Hunchback of Notre Dame*. (Not surprisingly neither of these lasted long in theatres that cost over 70,000,000 Euros each to build).

Theatres prop up ailing box-office returns with two-month summer seasons of third rate versions of *42ND Street, My Fair Lady, West Side Story*, etc., pumped into the German theatre economy specifically for the purpose. And yet, despite this ominous trend, the central debate among the critics is still that of Goethe's *Prolog im Theater* – Kunst v. Box Office with Kunst winning walls down.

Reputations and habits die hard. One of the strengths of the decentralised German system is that a theatre revolution could begin from any of those one hundred and thirty State theatres – the means of production are there to achieve it. But the East is desperately short of money and, increasingly, of artists, and the West is having to tighten its belt, an unaccustomed occupation, and hasn't caught up with the fact that, within the forseeable future, it is going to have to do something to justify the existence of its theatres. Some of these have a reputation gained some twenty years ago although the work has long ceased to mean anything.

Directors are still play-boys demanding impossible conditions and commanding impossible fees – the top ones £60,000 a production and, believe me, they have good accountants. The top actors in the system get paid some £100,000 and can still do TV and freelance work on top. This leads to what is known as Lufthansa theatre where Stuttgart, Leipzig, Vienna and Dusseldorf co-ordinate their respective repertoires with the help of a flight plan. Sometimes repertoire leaflets are only finalised some two weeks before a performance – hardly conducive to building up a healthy advance.

In the Ruhr, the Opera Houses of Wuppertal, Dortmund, Dusseldorf, Essen and Köln, sometimes have a tacit agreement to play only two nights a week, whenever possible, to avoid drawing on each others' audiences. Ballet companies and orchestras from different cities have already merged. There is little or no educational work in the big theatres and work for children and young people receives a surprisingly small share of the cake and is usually confined to the ubiquitous fairy story at Christmas. Front of House facilities are often non-existent – bars, catering, etc., – and, for many, marketing is a Mephistophelian device to promote capitalist culture. Bureaucracy is top-heavy and the ratio of people working behind the scenes to those in front is often as high as ten or twelve to one.

This smug and complacent attitude towards earned income extends as far as the box office. The ratio of subsidy to monied bums on seats is often as high as 90% to 10%. After all, why should we encourage people to come to the theatre? Theatre doesn't need audiences – it just needs artists – and, of course, subsidy. If there's a deficit, the State will pay it off. And the German critics despise box office success. If a one thousand seater is full every night, they reason, then there must be something wrong with the product. It must be *unterhaltung*-entertainment. Far better to rave and enthuse about a piece of tortuous esoteric post-modernism, a *Macbeth* where the play is unrecognizably performed by five actors speaking the wrong lines, which would be better off in a smaller more experimental place, more suited to the couple of hundred who attend.

In Germany, Shakespeare is considered a German playwright and compared with England there is ten times the amount of Bardic activity, most of the productions being much freer, more experimental and often deconstructed to death. (See above.) Each new Shakespeare production occasions a new translation. Consequently there are no standard texts other than the nineteenth century Schlegel/ Tieck or Eschenberg and, more recently, those of the late Erich Fried, all of whom are usually plundered as the basis for new versions, rather than being performed for themselves. (I plead guilty here.)

I have done eleven translations from English into German, including four Shakespeares. I work mainly with Gottfried and Inga Greiffenhagen. Gottfried is that rare thing – a genuine dramaturg. In this country we would call most German dramaturgs press officers, their function often being to research material for the extended play programmes that German theatres produce – books in themselves. Gottfried is in the great tradition of men of letters in the theatre, those who combine the talents of editor, researcher, adviser, selector, critic, producer, confidant, translator, philosopher. He is brilliantly receptive with a boundless, child-like enthusiasm, and totally unafraid of revising his opinion. A marvellous man and a great friend.

I am very pedantic working on Shakespeare in translation, attempting the impossible, insisting on the exact meaning and rhythm of a word or phrase. This frustrates Gottfried who feels that the talent of the translator lies in creatively interpreting the work in hand. This won't do for me. I'm a stickler for accuracy where Shakespeare is concerned, and no approximation will do. This often leads, I admit, to a constipated solution for some phrases that are virtually untranslatable but, ultimately, the bonus comes when one achieves in German the sharpness and accuracy of the language in English. Another bonus, if it can be looked on as such, is that, of necessity, the language of the translation has to be modern, even if one is consciously looking for phrases that are out of fashion or archaic. The mere fact that one is translating today and not in 1604, mostly if not automatically, disqualifies an authentic parallel linguistic equivalent. This gives great freedom to the translator and to the production. Actors and directors deal with a language that connects instantly with a contemporary audience without the barrier of anachronism in between. This is one of the reasons why there is so much more experimentation with Shakespeare abroad than there is in England. While we are stuck with the archaic mould of Elizabethan language, others treat the plays as living material, malleable, organic. They embrace the themes and ideas enthusiastically, transferring them to whatever culture is being explored in a fresh and often anarchic form. The freedom and release of creative energy that this brings is enviable. Shakespeare is much easier in translation. Though in Germany you would be pushed to acknowlege that.

Simplicity is simply not simple for the majority of Germans. But I do not know an actor alive who would rather have good notices and an empty theatre than bad notices and full ones. And the composition of audiences in both Staats- and Privattheaters is often alarming in itself. The cause is the 'Abonnement' system – subscription – where Patrons go the first Tuesday of each month, sit in the same seat that their Grandparents sat in, watching they don't know what. Average age sometimes one hundred and eighty. Unfortunately the spectator is treated with scant regard in the German State theatres (and in many another European country as well, one has to say). Members of the audience may travel hundreds of miles only to arrive and discover that, instead of Hartmann's *Hamlet* playing that night, it's a reading of the poems of Hölderlin. The postponing of first nights and cancelling of performances is legion for, unlike the British system, there is no method of understudying roles. With the addition of just this one simple working practice, millions of Euros would be saved each year. It's the fault of the big German directors, who, scared of the critics, rehearse unendingly until a play is merely undergoing a series of interminable run-throughs. And then, a kamikaze opening. No previews, bang. Unveil it.

For all this and for all that, when theatre happens in Germany – good theatre – there is excitement in the air. Theatre matters. People who make theatre matter. Unlike the British insular xenophobic system, there is an international cross-fertilisation of ideas and talents that only exists in Britain in opera. But one would have thought that, with the demolition of the East/West borders, more contact would have been made by our great British preservers and propagators of national culture. Indeed, the RNT under Sir Richard Eyre, Michael Billington, *Guardian* critic was able to write, had such a preoccupation with transatlantic writing that it is a wonder British Equity didn't allow it to form an American repertory company.

Yet we laugh and point a disparaging finger at the German system and say 'There you are, too much subsidy makes for poor art. A waste of tax payers money. I don't want my money spent on that rubbish!' Well, I'm a tax payer and I believe in the German way. Despite the shortcomings of the system Germany at least attempts to place the arts at the centre of society. As a taxpayer I want to spend more than 50p in tax (because that's all we're talking about) on culture in Britain. In our rejection of the arts as a basis for a healthy society (apart from allowing a select handful to graze the green, green grass of privilege) we present a pathetic picture alongside our Teutonic near-neighbours. It may be a long and painful process but I am convinced that Germany, as it does with all things, will find a way to come to terms with theatre in the twenty-first century that is productive, economic and of immense political and cultural importance. If the German system collapses (as some hope it will and some practitioners are helping it to) then there is little hope that we, in these islands, will ever witness the day when the arts will be seen as a service and not as a luxury.

End of diatribe.

20

Guardian Diary

'Villify! Villify! Some of it will stick!'.

In 1992 I resigned as Intendant (Chief Executive) of the Deutsches Schauspielhaus (National Theatre), Hamburg.

There came a point when I found myself with three libel suits on my hands. One against the *Suddeutsche Zeitung*, one against the *Frankfurter Algemeine*, and the third against the *Frankfurter Rundschau*. The equivalents of *The Times*, *The Telegraph* and *The Independant*.

German libel laws are very clear and codified. They conform to the Countercheck Quarrelsome, the Lie Circumstantial and the Lie Direct. Nobody gets any money, only degrees of apology. I won them all. It's not that I found the critics in Germany any more or less scathing about my work than they are in England; it was the depth of personal animosity that was frightening. I was a public figure, under constant scrutiny from the media, both locally and nationally. If I farted, it became a major news item, particularly as it was a Welsh one. Lies about my family, my income, my financial affairs, my personal life. I didn't quite have tenacious photographers crawling through half a mile of undergrowth on their stomachs to get a shot of my tits, or nocturnal audial voyeurs with twenty foot erections listening in on my private conversations, but close to.

I woke up one day and thought – 'Here I am in a foreign country, working in a language that is not my own, in a culture that is not my own, on my own. I don't need all this.' So I got out.

My final week as Intendant, December 1992.

Sunday 8th
Up at 7.00 a.m. to finish writing the laudatio oration for the Boy Gobert Prize, an award for the Best Young Actor and Best Young Actress for the year. This time it has been won by Susanne Schaefer and Marcus Bluhm, two of my company. A translation, done overnight, arrives in a taxi at 8.30. I spend one and a half hours on the phone discussing the details. To the Thalia Theater for 11 o'clock, Eight hundred dignitaries from the world of the arts and politics. I present two awful tin pins and a cheque each for five thousand marks. Marcus and Susanne are very nervous. They perform a terrible cabaret, but nobody minds. They are charming together, and wonderfully talented. I am very proud, having nurtured them both. Skip the lunch and walk around the Alster Lake with Patsy my wife. A shimmering, shining Hamburg afternoon. Cold, brown and green, the water glinting and still. Elegant houses reflecting a December orange sun. the green copper spires of this ancient free port thrusting for warmth up into the blue frost-white sky. Take Patsy to the airport and then go to the theatre to celebrate with Marcus and Susanne after their performance of 'Dancing at Lugnasa'.

Monday 9th
The first day of the *Technische Einrichtung* – fit up – of the set and lights of *The Ginger Man*, my final production, opening on the 14th. A dark grey abstract Georgian townscape of Dublin, designed by Chris Dyer. Rehearse with the actors upstairs in the grosse *Probebuehne* – the large rehearsal room. NDR film crew doing a documentary. Uli Tukur not on form. I send the film crew away. Onstage in the evening, with thirty extras and twelve

children, to rehearse complicated set changes of furniture, doors, and a mass of horse and hand pulled carts. (When will I ever have the chance to have a cast of forty-five actors again?) A nightmare. Nothing works. Retire to my office at 11.30 p.m. with Chris and John Leonard, sound designer, to drink a bottle of Jameson and think.

Tuesday 10th

The technical rehearsal proper, with no lighting and a concept that is bidding fair to be a disaster. 6.00 a.m. Meet with Nick Schliefer, my lighting designer. Australian with two German parents. Willing to give up his Australian nationality for German in order to work in England as an EEC passport holder. Something funny there. 10 o'clock, begin the battle of the revolve (I have got so used to calling it the *Drehscheibe* that it is only now that I can remember the English word) Manage by 11.00 p.m. to get through half the play, including a child and horse rehearsal. No break, nothing to eat. The most malnutritious period of a director's life. Pies and sandwiches on the run if at all. 11.30 p.m. Nick carries on rigging. We retire to my office to sink a bottle of Jameson and think, the numbers growing with the arrival of Malcolm Ranson, fight director.

Wednesday 11th

6.00 a.m. Working out a new chart for the set changes. I am going to have to abandon my original idea. Compromise time to get the show on at all. Carry on the technical rehearsal until 6 p.m. Don't complete the play. Will do a run ay 8.00 p.m. without the last two scenes. Meet in between in my office with the Maltese ambassador and the Chief Dramaturg from Weimar. An offer to do *Aida* in Cairo and a double English and German Schiller project in Malta and Weimar. Will talk about it if it happens. The run-through, as predicted, is total chaos. We don't finish, as predicted. A number of people have sneaked in to get a quick preview, including other directors. They sneak out again, shaking their heads. The profession should know better but never does. Midnight. Retire to the office to drink a bottle of Jameson and think.

Thurday 12th
6.00 a.m. Come to a decision. Ring Uli. We decide that the first night can only happen if a performance of *The Cherry Orchard*, due to take place on Friday night, is cancelled to allow us to work right through. Crazy German system, crazy scheduling, Our final dress rehearsal had been going to take place at 9.30 a.m. on Friday morning to allow time at 2 p.m. to change the sets over to *The Cherry Orchard*. The problem is partly my fault. Normally I leave time in the run up to a show for previews. Uli didn't want any so I decided to go with the other system knowing we were pushed for time. No previews, relinquishing the stage in the evening for another show. Disaster. Now it means turning away a full house on Friday night. Naturally Peter Raddatz, my administrator, is pretty sour. I also have to cancel a dinner arranged for me, late on Friday, by the *Freundes Kreis* – friends of the theatre. A farewell present. We work all day and I strip away unnecessary complicated technical problems. A full run through that evening. Miles better. The Schauspielhaus crew are tremendous, working on well past their normal hours. We know now we can do it. Retire to the office with the company till 3.00 a.m. to go through notes and possible cuts and sink several bottles of everything. A certain sense of euphoria in the air.

Friday 13th
Work all day further simplifying set changes. Final dress rehearsal. With even further technical tightening on the Saturday and if Uli keeps his nerve, there is a show. Retire to the Dorf, local inn of

Thespian repute, to sink a couple of bottles and in that silly state of overtiredness where you spend two hours flipping beer mats over and catching them. I manage nineteen. All the best thinking is done that way. 3.30 a.m. Bed.

Saturday 14th

A sense of excitement in the air. Not a seat to be had in the one thousand three hundred and fifty seater for weeks. The largest seating capacity in Germany. Critics from all over Europe for final production. Stockholm, Copenhagen, Berlin, Brussels, Paris, Vienna, Budapest, Amsterdam. None from England. J. P. Donleavy, the author, stranded at Heathrow, on his way over from Dublin, due to fog. Doesn't get to the premiere. Maybe that's what happened to the English critics. However as none of them had given any indication of coming, I don't give them the benefit of the doubt. During the show, drank a lot of wine in the office. I never watch first nights. Occasionally sneak a look at what's going on on closed circuit TV. Reception at the end ecstatic. Roars of cheers for the actors. Marian Brechwoldt, a wonderfully dirty, lusty Mary, doing things on stage that actors don't dare do in England. Marlen Diekhoff, Burchart Klauser, Katrin Striebeck and of course Uli Tukur, one of the most exciting young actors in the world today. Donleavy had been overawed by him in rehearsal. And JP is a man who has seen both Nicol Williamson and Richard Harris in the role. I go on stage, as is the custom, expecting that the booers would be out in force. A pleasant surprise. Only a couple, drowned out by the cheers. All the staff and technicians on stage taking a bow. Chaos. Drink with the crew on stage afterwards to say goodbye. Off to the celebration at midnight, which also coincides with my birthday. About one thousand people are there. Sometimes the first night parties are bigger than the first night audience. Enter to a sea of waving candles, the room lit up like a Christmas tree, and resounding applause. I am lifted up onto a table, but I can't speak. The moment is too much. The Minister for Culture, Dr Christina Weiss makes a speech thanking me for my work and presents me with a gift from the City of Hamburg, a meticulously wrapped silver flat quadrate parcel which looks and feels suspiciously like a CD. It is a CD. Of Mahler's *Fifth*. Thirty marks worth. Ten marks for each year of my tenancy.

A director's life is worth a lot.

Somebody has made a wonderful 3 tier cake with the names inscribed on it of the eleven shows that I have produced in Hamburg since 1985. We party through the night, me mostly in my office, people coming and going, never less than fifty, the music ringing out into the dawn from fiddle, pipe, banjo and bohran. A man playing a tin tray. Turns out to be a Dubliner. 6 a.m. Down to the harbour front to a bar, the Baton Rouge, Uli Tukur leading the way. On into the morning. Packing, cleaning up. 4.00 p.m. The party moves back to the Schauspielhaus. My official farewell. Two hundred people, the board of the theatre, journalists, the city of Hamburg, theatre staff, friends, TV and radio crews, all asking the same question: Why am I going? A stack of presents. Very emotional but a warm glow. 8.00 p.m. Move to the Dorf Bar which Tuschi has opened up especially. About one hundred people pass through. The cake which has travelled from the first night party, to the farewell, and now to here, is finally cut, everyone choosing a slice of their favourite show – Hamlet tying with Reineke Fuchs. More speeches, more tears. Claus Pohl, playwright, makes a witty attack on the philistines of Hamburg and falls out into the night. I haven't eaten since Friday or slept since 6.00 a.m. Saturday. To the sound of singing and the sight of candles waving I sneak home to bed at 3.00 a.m.

Monday 16th
Back in the office at 9.00 a.m. to clear out. 11 a.m. My final press

conference. Packed, I am too tired to talk coherently in German. For the first and last time I give it in English. A retrospective of what I have and haven't achieved at the Deutsches Schauspielhaus. Say some pretty hard things about German Kulturpolitik. But I love the Schauspielhaus, the people who work in it and most of all the actors and the Hamburg audience. I also have a few records to point to in income and audience attendance. I see a little shit of an NDR Radio journalist, who has vilified me since I came to Hamburg, sitting in the audience. I decide not to punch him on the nose and answer the same question again. Why am I leaving? Retire to the office for a last drink with a few close friends. Learn that Donleavy had eventually made it to Hamburg on the Sunday, couldn't find the party and spent the day train spotting at the Hauptbahnhof, and was e'en now winging his way back to Dublin. An 'I wish' story. I, too, am on my way now to the airport, driven by Wolfgang, my personal assistant and friend. Fly to Heathrow to join Patsy on a flight to Dublin to celebrate our Silver Wedding on the morrow.

21
Powerplay

I returned to Germany four years later to direct *'Tis Pity She's a Whore* at the Schauspielhaus in Cologne at the invitation of the Intendant Günter Krämer, later also General Intendant of both the Theatre and the Opera in Cologne. It was a nightmare.

Rehearsals had been split, three weeks at the fag end of the season in June before picking the production up again in October. The German system often operates in this manner – rehearsing a couple of shows before the summer break, to open the new season three months later. For me personally a frustrating work method – production *interruptus*. I hate it.

The staff and actors had been following Günter around for years, as is the German way, and were used to his methods. They certainly couldn't get used to mine. In June it was frazzled, end of season blues. In November, freezing fog and flu. At one point Günter called me into his office and said that there had been a deputation from the actors asking him to look at the show. He had a suggestion to make. He had (unknown to me) watched a rehearsal between Putana and Arrabella. He thought he knew what was wrong. He would take a rehearsal of the scene, the whole company would be there and he would demonstrate the style in which the scene and the play should be directed.

I was flabbergasted. This 'young upstart' was suggesting that he should show me how to direct? I didn't know what to say. I wasn't exactly setting the town on fire, but the production wasn't in that kind of trouble. I recognised the ploy for what it was –

German powerplay between directors. A common gambit. I thanked Günter very much and said I thought that I should first of all try and work the problem out for myself, but that if I found I couldn't then, rest assured, I would come and ask him to sort things out for me.

The next round was a grim-faced meeting with all the technical staff and Herr Krämer. The Technical Director stated that there were thirty-four scene changes, some of them lasting up to three minutes. He estimated that the show would have over an hour added to its running time merely through the time it took to change scenes. Chris Dyer (the designer) and I laughed, amazed. None of the scene changes, we said, would last longer than fifteen seconds and some would overlap.

They laughed. These crazy British.

The long and short of it was that the technical staff were refusing to do the show. It would appear that under Günter they had got used to doing shows that needed no scene changes at all. This British method was all very old-fashioned. A real bed! A real piano! A real altar! I said they could all take a holiday as far as I was concerned, I would do the work with the twenty-four *Statisten* (extras) who constituted the gangs, waiters, street people, etc., in the production. The entire theatre could watch a demonstration. And I called on Peter Theiss to organise it all. Peter had been a student at The Hamburger Hochschule of Theater and had done a similar thing for me on both *Hamlet* and *The Ginger Man* at the Schauspielhaus and, although only a *Statist* himself, had a natural organisational authority.

The appointed time arrived. There were twenty-six of them in the stalls, the complete *Technische Leitung* (technical department) and hangers on, to watch the debacle. I chose the most difficult scene change to begin with, taking off-stage the huge bed, altar, candles and crucifix and wheeling on the grand piano, sofa, dining table and chairs all of which had to go off and come from the same small, up-stage entrance – a sliding panel under a balcony. The stage was also steeply raked on an angle.

Peter had organised them all brilliantly. The first run at it took fifteen seconds. The second twelve. I turned round. The stalls were empty. They had all slunk away without a murmur. That was the end of that.

The following day yet another incident occurred of the kind that convinces me that the Sagittarian star under which I was born decided to make life as difficult as possible for someone it considered a bolshie little shit. 'These things are sent to try us', was my mother's favourite phrase.

The Queen was on her first state visit to Germany in about twenty years and was holding a banquet at the Augustusburg Palace in Bruehl, some twenty kilometres south of Köln, to which, as a leading figure in the arts in Germany (that is, former), I was invited. I asked Günter Krämer if I could use his car and driver to take me there. Up to this point he had been enormously generous with the use of his Intendant's facilities, insisting on me being driven everywhere by his chauffeur. This was the first time I had approached him to ask for such a favour. To my surprise, despite the fact that his car wasn't in use that night, Günter himself being in rehearsal, he refused with quite a huffy air. I shrugged and went off to phone a taxi. He was obviously trebly miffed that his power play hadn't worked, his technical crew had been bested and – na-na-na-na-nah – I had an invitation to dine with the Queen and he hadn't.

I rehearsed until quite late, rushed into my (hired) tux and waited for the taxi, on a Noah's Ark of a night.

It didn't come. I rang. It was on its way. I waited. I rang again. It was on its way.

I was getting anxious. It was 5.30. I was due there for 7.00.

At last the doorbell rang. I went downstairs.

Now normally the taxis are sleek, beige beasts, Mercedes that purr silently along at 180mph. This was an elephant of a white van, built to take about a hundred, with a traction engine of an exhaust. Could I arrive to meet Her Majesty in this? I had no choice, it was late and bucketing down. I climbed in.

'Where to?'

I must have found the only taxi driver in the world who didn't know where Bruehl and the Augustusburg Palace were.

Instead of taking the motorway he drove at ten miles an hour along the Landstrasse, stopping every five minutes to ask the way. The answer was always the same – just keep straight on. I was getting more and more desperate, time was ticking on, but there was no way of getting him out of second gear.

At last the Palace hove into view – a massive edifice rising out of the parkland, ablaze with light. How could this fool not have known? Taxis and limos were queuing to drive up the mile long approach, however the guards took one look at our tank and wouldn't let us through. I had to get out in the pouring rain, no coat and have a thorough frisking. At last I was allowed through – walking.

The driveway was lined with impassive cadets, all brandishing flaming torches in the pouring rain. I trudged shamefaced past them up the mile long drive, Bentleys, Rolls, taxis and Mercedes passing by, spraying me with wet and mud, the only drowned rat of a guest arriving at Augustusburg Palace on foot to meet the Queen. I had no idea how I would get back, I obviously hadn't rebooked the bus.

At last I collapsed into the foyer and went to check-in my little black bag. I wouldn't do that, said the lady, take it in with you – you never know who's been invited. Quite right. You wouldn't want the King of Spain swiping your credit card.

I went into the great reception hall with the two thousand others. We lined up to climb the magnificent double staircase and shake the royal and other hands – Lizzie, Phil, Chancellor Kohl, President Weizecker and wife – and went into dinner.

On the table were two bottles of Königschaffhausen Spaetburgunder, from Baden. I was intrigued that on such an important occasion they were serving German red wine, in those days almost a contradiction in terms. It was delicious. It must be very special.

I was at the table with Charles Anscombe, the Queen's private secretary and press representative, and sitting with the Lady Mayor of Bonn on one side, and the head of Krupp on the other. Amazing what you have in common with the head of the largest arms firm in Europe and the civic leader of the (then) German capital. Anscombe was very indiscreet, regaling us with many a boudoir anecdote, and the wine was delicious and flowing copiously – it must have cost a fortune.

Post meal we were to mingle in the state rooms for coffee and meet the Queen informally. Coffee, yes. Tea nowhere to be seen, merely a host of shrugging waiters. Then I saw a well groomed lady precariously balancing a cup and saucer and asked where she had obtained it. 'Through that door there', she said. 'Follow me.' Through the door we went, nothing but a long corridor with rooms leading off. Eventually reached the kitchen, 'This gentleman would like some tea', she said, flashed a smile and disappeared. I thanked her and, tea supplied, made my way back.

I found the only person I knew there, the German director Peter Palitzsch, and regaled him with the story. Who was the lady, he asked? No idea – that one over there. I pointed. Oh, that's Hannalore Kohl. I had only been taken to the kitchens by the wife of the Bundeskanzler.

I fought my way over to apologise for not knowing. 'Think nothing of it', she said. 'It drives me mad at these things. They always assume that the whole world drinks only coffee. I've been on at Helmut about it for years.'

There was a huge fellow in breeches, white dicky-bow and a red waistcoat doing the rounds, tapping people on the shoulder and leading them over to meet Ma'am. I felt such a tap and turned round.

'Your name sir', he said bending low to catch it.

'Michael Bogdanov.'

He straightened up and beckoned me with a finger. I followed.

Her Majesty was surrounded by four or five dignitaries with chains. We waited. Then – 'Michael Bogdanov, Ma'am, ex-Intendant of the Deutsches Schauspielhaus, Hamburg and Artistic Director of the English Shakespeare Company.'

Unbelievable. Two thousand guests and he must have known the background of every one. Her Majesty smiled, then said in that inimitable voice of hers, said –

'Oah, The English Shekespeare Company. Tanks end guns.' (She had seen *The Henrys* trilogy at the Old Vic)

After ten a gong sounded and we were all ushered like sheep out of the rooms. Of course I hadn't had the foresight to order a taxi to replace the traction engine. Won't get one now, said the bag lady helpfully, they've all been booked. Best walk to the village and get one locally. How far? About a kilometre from the gates.

Back down the drive I went, everything in reverse. Mercifully it had stopped raining. I turned left and carried on. One kilometre? Four. I got to the village about midnight. Everything was shut. I found a phone box, got a local taxi number and then . . . no change. Only a fifty mark note. Almost crying I wandered around trying to find a house with a light still on. Nothing. I went back to the phone box and waited. Success! A figure shambled towards me.

'Excuse me, could you change a fifty mark note?' He mumbled something and shot away like a startled rabbit. Another twenty minutes. A man approached. I rushed out an explanation before he had time to think. I can't change the note he said, but have a couple of marks on the house. And he gave me some coins. I could have kissed him. No reply from the first two numbers, then a sleepy voice answered the third. What time do you bloody call this? I explained. A lot of grumbling and shouting at someone the other end. 'I'll be there in half an hour.'

'Half and hour?'

I shouted 'Can't you . . .', but he was gone. I huddled in the box for warmth, teeth chattering, nose a bluer shade of purple. Forty-five minutes later he arrived and in silence we drove back to Köln, charged me one hundred marks for the privilege.

It was 3 a.m. My audience with the Queen was over.

The next day I searched all Köln for some Königschaffhausen Spaetburgunder, but so rare was it that my search was wineless. Then someone suggested I try a little Baden wine bar on the second floor of a building round the corner. And yes, they had some! How much, I asked. Six marks fifty a bottle, about £2.25. Very special. And the castle must have bought it in bulk for about five marks. I was deeply impressed that instead of plying the guests with Petrus and Latour they had chosen a really cheap German wine on which to get everybody smashed. I bought a case.

I didn't offer Krämer any but I should have taken him up on his offer to redirect the play. It was one of the worst pieces of work I have ever done.

22

A Letter to WS on the Occasion of his Birthday

Dear Will,

I am sorry to land you with this on your birthday, but isn't it about time we stuck your plays in a trunk and locked them in the attic for about twenty years? I know it's not your fault, but your work has generated a whole farcical world-wide industry of pontificating critical academia. Why couldn't you have written your plays down properly in the first place, then we wouldn't have this crazy carousel of circus clowns fighting and writing about where the comma should really be? I know, I know – you were just a man of the theatre doing your thing, but do you think that it's easy to explain that to a 21st century Ivy League/Oxbridge academic? And a few notes on character and motivation wouldn't have gone amiss, then we wouldn't have Cabinet Ministers like Osborne triumphantly trotting out quotes about law and order to back the belief that you were a high Tory.

Who's Osborne? It's not worth explaining. You see, they think that you are one of them, the Oxbridge bunch. I know – it's a joke. How could they so misunderstand you? Easy. They ignore the difficult political bits – the pacifism, the humanism, the feminism – call the plays they don't understand 'problem' plays.

No, Pericles isn't performed very much these days. I'm afraid that we're down to about half a dozen pot boilers, curriculum driven. No, nobody studies Latin and Greek anymore – just

Romeo and Juliet over and over again. Most of your other plays are rapidly being ghettoised. Can't afford them, you see. And you really wouldn't recognise the theatres and the audiences either. Very comfortable, very cosy, very middle-class. Nor would you understand the way a lot of actors speak your lines. Very boring. Except for the Africans and the Indians. Oh, yes, and the kids. You work in translation though. The Germans think of you as one of them.

And where have you buried the conclusive proof that the plays are yours? It's driving me crazy arguing with all these clowns who think you didn't write any of the stuff. Who? The Earl of Oxford for one. I know he died in 1604, twelve years before you did. Ridiculous isn't it? Yes, of course he was a third rate poet, but apparently he wrote, *Lear, Macbeth, Othello, The Tempest* and ten others all before 1604, stockpiled them and then somehow after his death got someone to release them one by one until 1616!

Who? There was a film called *Anonymous* a few years back says it was Ben Johnson. I know – the bastard. Mind, he wrote nice things about you in your *Collected Works*. They can't understand where you got your knowledge you see – Greek, Latin, Chemistry, Biology, Italy etc., etc.,. Of course you were an avid reader, anyone can see that (though *Anonymous* didn't even think you were educated enough to write your own name! (Why are your signatures all so different? I've often wondered. . . .) And it doesn't help that you filched a load of material from other writers – Ovid, Montaigne, Holinshed, North's Plutarch. Sure, I know, everybody was at it – it's why you didn't keep any of your drafts. Who wants some other bum writer claiming the plays are theirs. . . .

Who else? Kit Marlowe for one. Evidently he didn't die in that pub brawl in Deptford: he escaped to France and spent the next twenty five years writing the plays and sending them back to England. No, I don't know how anybody could stand by for

A Letter to WS on the Occasion of his Birthday

twenty-five odd years and watch somebody else take the credit and reap the fame for producing thirty-eight masterpieces, becoming filthy rich in the process. It's not human nature is it really? Maybe one or two possibly, but thirty-eight?

Who else? Loads of them, seventy-eight at the last count – I won't bore you. Oh very well – Francis Bacon. Yes, incredible isn't it. His own stuff is so convoluted, erudite, and up its own arse there's no similarity at all.

But let's face it, Will, even if you did write the plays – no, no, don't worry, I'm a fervent believer – you're just not popular any more (were you ever?). You've become a cultural collectible, not even studied in some schools. Oh yes, there is a live popular culture – football, Karaoke, drag, strip, pop, stand-up. Stand up? It's like a load of Falstaffs let loose to rap about sex and politics. You would love it. But I'm afraid that for 99% of the population you are totally irrelevant. On TV in 2012 the Olympics, were watched by twenty-five thousand viewers, but a few years back only half a million watched *Measure for Measure*, your marvellous analysis of corruption and sleaze in government. TV – television – moving, talking pictures on a small screen: you would love that too. And film – ditto on a large one. A lot of people think that's where you would be working if you were alive now. I'm not so sure . . . modern adaptations are great but some of the other attempts . . . well. Unfortunately TV has dealt you a bunch of hefty blows over the years. Apart from *The Hollow Crown* recently that is. Yes, a bunch of the Historys, *Richard II*, the *Henry IV*s and *Henry V*, which were about as good as it gets. These days it's all cooking, gardening, shagging – you name it. Get me out of here. Shagging? Didn't you invent the word? It's what happens as a consequence of 'groping for trouts in a peculiar river': I always liked that description of yours.

Oh yes, and you'd have a Facebook page – and a billion followers on Twitter. (It's too difficult to explain). It's this technological thing you see. These days we can order you up electronically on Kindle – a sort of storage library that you can keep in your pocket. Unfortunately in fifty years time you'll probably be out of print you see – iTunes? iPods? New Media just made for you.

So, Will, what do you think? Ban all activity for twenty years? Hope that the plays will emerge sparkling fresh into the mid century light? It probably wouldn't work. The last time the theatres were closed in 1640 for that length of time the Establishment wasn't long in getting a fresh grip on its Willy.

No, I expect your plays will simply suffer a slow linguistic death by attrition until only those who study them will be able to understand them. Maybe we should translate you into modern English. Why not? We do it with Beowulf and Chaucer. Not a very happy birthday, Will. Turn in your grave.

P.S. I'm sorry about the RSC.

23

Critics – Payback time

'If I die – I forgive you: If I live – we shall see'.

(Spanish proverb)

It was January, 1969, my first ever production in London, the opening production of The Theatre Upstairs at The Royal Court, *A Comedy of the Changing Years* by David Cregan. It was nowing, bitterly cold and the Georgian windows had not yet been filled in. We rehearsed in gloves and duffle-coats, huddled round a small blow-heater, the only warmth that the theatre would provide. The opening night the critics struggled up the hundred and one stairs, complaining bitterly. One turned back altogether. Philip Hope-Wallace refused to sit in his allocated place and dumped himself deliberately behind a pillar, unable to see the action. Milton Shulman sat in the front row, legs stretched out in front of him, occasioning the actors to step over them during the performance, and talked loudly throughout to B.A. Young. Harold Hobson went to sleep before the performance began and only woke up at the applause. It was my first experience of London critics.

Why be a director? If a new play is successful, it's the author; if it fails, it's the director. If an actor surpasses themselves, theirs is the credit; if they give a bad performance – the fault is the production's. A designer produces a highly visual set that, spatially and practically, is well nigh impossible to operate on and the entire rehearsal period revolves around ways to negotiate this monstrosity, papering over the cracks, compromising on staging in order to give the impression that the whole production is organic. (Don't ask me how this happens, but it sometimes does.) The result?

'The director fails to take the opportunities offered by X's stunning use of the stage, supplying instead a clumsy, under-rehearsed, mish-mash of half-realised ideas and inept staging.'

An actor incorporates three back-somersaults into his perform-ance, only to end up on stage encased in a suit of armour (don't ask me how it gets to this stage before you catch up with what the costume designer has been up to, but it does). Rehearsals and previews go a bomb, the audiences are peeing in the aisles. The first night nose-dives, the actors panic and lose their rhythm, the comedy is forced, friends laugh too loud and in the wrong places, critics don't laugh at all.

'The production is about as funny as a fart. The director should take a lesson out of X's book and learn about rhythm, subtlety and timing.'

Occasionally something hurts.

'Bogdanov and Behan, a marriage made in hell', (Alistair Macauley, *The Hostage*).

'An exercise in noisy desperation . . . Bogdanov's apparent lack of interest in the play', (Sheridan Morley, *The Venetian Twins*.)

'A director who gives the impression that he'd find the 'Carry On' films an intellectual challenge', (Charles Spencer – *Faust I* and *II*).

Sometimes it is hard to believe that critics have seen the same show.

'One to miss', *What's On* of *Shakespeare on the Estate*, which collected a BAFTA, a Royal Society of Television and a Banff Film Festival Award.)

The cold comfort is that, as long as critics are split down the middle, at least something evidently is happening.

Any fool can criticise and many of them do. My main criticism of critics is not that they dislike my work (and anyway, not all of them do), but that they possess an appalling lack of vision. If the stage holds the mirror up to nature (I'll beg that question for the moment), then it seems that in Britain the critic holds a very opaque mirror up to the stage. Accordingly, the critic is two stages removed from life. The critic reacts to art reacting to life. Now, put like that, it sounds just about right – an analysis of the way that a piece of work measures up to the subject it is tackling. But in reality it doesn't work like that at all. Life – art – criticism, is not a straight line. That way artificiality and pretension, superficiality, false values interpose themselves between the subject and the critic. Life – art – criticism is a triangle, with the critic at the apex, with two umbilical chords, one to life, one to art. This is not to accord the critic the pride of place in this troilic configuration. If we were to draw an authorial triangle, the writer would occupy the same position in relation to life and art. Ditto the actor. Whoever, wherever the artist, they must be attached unseverably to life itself. From the standpoint of the critic, one line must lead to life as she is lived and the other must lead onwards and upwards to the future, not merely the future of the art form in hand, but the future of the community, the country, the world.

In other words, the critic has a duty to point the way forward. This involves commitment on the part of the critic, a cleaving to an ideology against which all theatre is measured. (Dear, oh dear, that most un-english thing, a political viewpoint.) This does not mean measuring everything on the Richter frivolity scale, dismissing out of hand those things we would class as entertainment (*Unterhaltungstheater* the German theatre critics sniffily term it, scathingly totalling the exuberant audience-pleaser with a few well chosen words running to twenty-five columns), but it does mean getting behind the result of a production to investigate and appreciate the intention of a piece of work, before measuring how far short it falls of that intention.

Now all critics would say that that is exactly what they do, but the actuality is somewhat different. In Irving Wardle's otherwise excellent book on the function of the critic entitled 'Theatre Criticism', nowhere is there a statement of his actual raison d'etre. Wardle, a rare enthusiast I hasten to add, was concerned more with the art of reviewing (a term he uses consistently), rather than criticism. His theory is one of reaction – nothing is pro-active. The critic as reporter.

In that case, why be a critic at all? Who are you satisfying? Who are you helping? Or, are you merely encouraging the artistic aspirations of the chattering classes, forming an elite coterie, an incestuous Masonic lodge of a dozen or so chums, part of the Oxbridge conspiracy? Where is the passion of the great reformers? The critics of the past were not merely interested in poetics and aesthetics, they were interested in the way the world wags, in producing a game play for life. It's no use quoting Aristotle, Sophocles, Schlegel, Hegel, Hazlitt and Hunt without acknowledging that passion. Shaw and Tynan had one thing in common, theatre is about change. Criticism should be about helping that change.

'In England we have come to rely on a comfortable time lag of fifty years or a century intervening between the perception that something ought to be done and a serious attempt to do it.' This was H G Wells almost one hundred years ago. Our critic should just about be entering the 21st century any time now . . .

Directing is a lonely affair. The odds of failure are stacked so heavily against you. Six months of tortuous preparation work and rehearsal can go up in the smoke in the space of a couple of hours, the victim of technical adversity, actor nerve-loss and November fog. When people get bronchitis, they don't go to the doctor, they go to the theatre. Because an audience only sees the finished product, it has relatively little or no knowledge of how that finished result has been arrived at. Ditto critics. And, if a critic has attended rehearsals, it disqualifies him or her from writing about the production. Too much knowledge destroys the objective appraisal of the finished result.

A few years back, Michael Billington found it a revelation when he directed a piece of work, Marivaux's *The Will* at the RSC.

'What have I learned from the rehearsal process? Many things: . . . directing is a process of constant adjustment . . . a matter of discovering the route rather than imposing the destination . . . Many of the problems are pragmatic . . . Every day the project changes like a living organism.' What is annoying and frustrating about all that is that Mr B had got that far as a critic without realising or understanding any of those things. It doesn't say much for some of the others. (It may seem that I have a thing about Michael Billington – it's just that I read *The Guardian* daily, even when abroad).

I am not advocating a system of semiotics; I do not believe that the creation of a new language of terminology to identify the component linguistic parts of text and performance can ever be anything other than an academic exercise in exclusivity. Certainly there is no way that lexemes and docastic modalities will ever be absorbed into the practitioners booklet. No. What I would like to see is critics undergo a course of practical theatre, the graft and grind of directing, to enable them to have a better understanding of how theatre happens and who is responsible for what. It might help dispel some of the theories about direction that are based purely on literary analysis. There are as many ways of directing as there are directors. Qualitative judgements such as 'disciplined' or 'undisciplined' as praise or criticisms might disappear. Stein can be disciplined and boring; Zadek could be undisciplined and exciting. Which one reaches further down into the trouser pocket? Some of the coins in Zadek's productions may have fallen out through the holes, but at least the hand could feel the balls.

In Britain, playwrights are far more willing than directors to take up cudgels in defence of their work. In Continental Europe directors engage in long running battles in print with art editors when the latter go on the attack. You always know when you have done a good or a bad piece of work and very rarely does a critic write something perceptive that hasn't struck you before. You are usually aware of the faults and holes in a production long before anybody gets to write about it.

Which brings me to my production of Goethe's *Faust*.

The critical reception that Faust received at the RSC in 1996/97 is a major reason why, in 1998, I abandoned London and returned to my native Wales to pursue film and TV in Cardiff and Theatre in Germany – though later I formed at the request of Swansea City Council, The Wales Theatre Company to produce large scale projects to tour Wales, operating out of The Grand theatre, Swansea.

As it happens this was my fourth exploration of Goethe's *Faust*, an obsession since my days at University. The first was a promenade version (the term had yet to be invented) in 1972 in the Gulbenkian Studio at the Newcastle Playhouse. Audience participation and debate, simultaneous action, the form was much influenced by The Living Theatre's productions of *Paradise Now* and *Antigone*.

The second was a Punk Rock musical version at the Young Vic Theatre in 1980 with Jim Carter reprising his Mephistopheles role from eight years earlier, written in conjunction with Jamie Reid. The third was an adaptation for The English Shakespeare Company's educational branch in 1992 of the Ulm Puppet play – the Ur-version of *Faust* – with magnificent carved wooden puppets from Jactito.

In other words the text and themes of Goethe's opus were not unknown to me.

Why is it that, whenever faced with a virtually unknown classic, our flock of Oxbridge chums cram noisily into the Penguin Introduction pen and huddle together for common literary warmth?

Here they wrote of Goethe's 'majestic awe' (six times); 'redemption and optimism' (seven times); 'awe' on its own, fourteen. The talk was of 'soaring poetry' (five times) when Goethe wrote three quarters of a twelve hour piece in Knittelvers, which roughly translated means 'vulgar doggerel'. Two critics – Coveney and de Jongh – even managed to write reviews without once mentioning Mephistopheles – the largest role in Western theatre otherwise and universally acknowledged to be a stunning tour de force from Hugh Quarshie. And they expect artists to take them seriously?

The problem, however, with peddling a traditionally received opinion of Goethe's *Faust* is that views have changed radically since the war. Nobody in Germany now dreams of talking about Goethe's optimism and the last production with such an ending was Gustav Grundgens' famous one during the war in Berlin. If *Part II* is performed at all, the redemption is cut and they send the bugger to hell. Why? They realised that the megalomaniacal thirst for power that led Faust to kill off an innocent family, ruin a country with hyper inflation, destroy another with war and sectarian violence, incinerate an old couple who stood in the way of his land development (shades of Donald Trump in land grab in Scotland), engage in piracy and destruction on the high seas, press-gang into slavery thousands of workers, many of whom were killed and maimed in the process – not to mention cloning experiments to produce a genetically pure race, all this led to Nietzsche, Schopenhauer, the *übermensch* philosophy and the justification of Germany's Imperialist ambitions of the last one hundred years. German soldiers even went into battle in World Wars I and II with copies of *Faust* in their knapsacks.

Optimism? Faust's soul is saved by the *ewigweibliche* – the love of a good woman? 'Sorry Adolf, it's the hot tongs for you.'

'But Eva loves me!' –

'Oh, that's all right then, come on up.'

No, boys and girls, you can't talk of Faust's redemption and

Goethe's optimism without taking on board these things. The Penguin Introduction is no help to you here. Read the play, preferably in the original, and then let's talk about it. For many people believe that Goethe was caught in a trap of his own making. Fifty years earlier he had written a scene where God promises to save Faust. When he finally came to the end, almost on his death bed, Goethe realised that he had created a fascist monster. The excuse that Faust should be saved because he was always searching, striving, didn't wash. On the other hand he, Goethe, the great man, couldn't die with the world believing him an atheist. So he saved Faust's soul on the flimsiest of pretexts, whipped him away from under Mephistopheles nose by the dubious device of angels seducing him with their bare bums and inflaming homosexual desire (stage direction – 'they drive him into the audience') and wrote a huge thirty minute Catholic mass to celebrate it. He then sealed the manuscript and popped off, leaving the world to cope with it after his death.

Professor Jane Brown, Goethe expert at the University of Washington, leads the field in believing the end to be ironic. Having worked on the play for six months Howard Brenton and I came to the same conclusion. A considered conclusion, chaps. Yet, from some, I was showered with dog's abuse as if I were the one who did not know the play.

* * *

I once had an interesting encounter with Nicholas de Jongh. He wrote in the *Guardian*, 'Although it looks as if Bogdanov has done something radical with *Henry V*, the production is, in truth, conservative, traditional and not that consistent.'

Here was something that was perceptive. The problem was one of two actors (John Dougall and Michael Pennington) sharing the central part.

Michael and I had developed the ruthless, imperialist side of

Hal, conquering Katherine in the final scene as a political necessity, a symbol of conquered France. John was more in the romantic Olivier mould, managing to turn the final scene into an affirmation of status quo thinking. Nicholas had seen John in the part. I rang him up, unusually, to talk about his review. I think he was astonished when I told him I thought his assessment was accurate. (I knew from the silence at the end of the phone when I said my name that he thought he was going to be metaphorically or literally punched on the nose.) I invited him to see a performance of *Henry V* with Michael playing Henry and then to say if he still felt the same. If he did, I admitted, then we had got something (or something had gone) radically wrong. I had a genuine desire to know his opinion.

I invited him to a note session on *The House of York, Part 2* of our compilation of the *Henry VIs*, to show him how things were still changing. He arrived and must have been fairly – what? – impressed? at the degree of genuine democratic debate. The nature of the work and the company had led people to be completely open about each other's work. On this particular afternoon, among many other things, he witnessed Charlie Dale relinquish a small role and a speech to Ben Bazell, on the arrival of the Duke of York from Ireland, in order to clarify the story. We lost an anonymous soldier from the scene in order to build up the character of Norfolk (Ben). It would happen that night. It is at moments like this, when theatre is fluid, changing, continually being reassessed, that I feel the true power it exerts over me. The challenge of the times.

Unfortunately, Nicholas never did see Michael P in *Henry V*, so I shall never know whether he would still have thought there was an inherent imbalance in the production or not. I should send him a DVD.

* * *

From John Peter's Article in
The Sunday Times – Romeo and Juliet:
'User-friendly tosh'

Shakespeare is not our contemporary. In the 1960s it became fashionable to think he was: the Bard emerged, cheery, laid-back and approachable, from academic gloom and from the tradition of old-fashioned acting.

This was not altogether a bad idea. It was important, and still is, that people should be able to recognise something of themselves in Shakespeare's characters; otherwise, listening to oddly dressed actors spouting blank verse becomes a wearisome cultural obligation, like museum-going for schoolchildren.

The intellectual excitement of such productions as Peter Hall's Hamlet in 1965, with David Warner in a college scarf, is not the realisation that Shakespeare was a Warwickshire Sartre born before his time, but that he was an Elizabethan with things to say which could engage someone in the mid 20th century who had read Sartre. You were quite clear in your mind that this writer was not your contemporary; your estimation of him shot up precisely because, from a distance of nearly 400 years, he was saying things that still made urgent sense. This is how drama can absorb the past into the present and expand your horizons.

The trouble with Michael Bogdanov's vulgar, messy and bone-crushingly boring English Shakespeare Company's production of Romeo And Juliet (Lyric, Hammersmith) is that it is hell-bent on making Shakespeare contemporary and on cheering you up, rather as the pub bore thumps you on the back and tells you that there's nothing complicated about the ERM, Squire, it's just a question of how many deutschmarks you get for your quid, right? Listen, Bogdanov seems to say, this Shakespeare stuff is easy. Romeo And Juliet has a lot of guts, a great story, it's a play about kids, kids like you, kids today, right, the whole kids and parents thing, repressive society and all the violence. It's got a lot of action and some great fights. Great.

What you actually get is a production wheezing desperately under the strain of topicality. Bogdanov impoverishes and vulgarises

Shakespeare by pushing and shoving him into the 20th century. The idea seems to be that if the Prince of Verona comes on wearing dark pebble glasses, the kids will accept him more easily; and that you will understand better that Mercutio is having a hangover if you see him putting Alka-Seltzer in his wine. The play has a sense of young people being doomed by hostile fate and their own headstrong passion: the production has none.

The whole tedious masquerade reeks of the busy down-market anxiety that Shakespeare should be made more user-friendly by generous applications of 'comic' business and as many diversions as possible, in case people should get bored or depressed by the words. The Tybalt-Mercutio duel is played mostly for laughs; it goes on for ages; the two men even stop for drinks; and a grotesque-looking old man prances around and between them, beating time on a pair of bongo drums. Mercutio mimes masturbation on a champagne bottle held against his groin and sprinkles the grateful citizens with the exploding foam. Capulet dictates his comments on the lovers' death to a comic-looking reporter, and there is a long dumbshow in which the main characters get photographed against the lovers' golden statues. The verse speaking, throughout the production, is dire.

In other words, this is the worst kind of director's theatre: not one in which the actor is asked to give a performance to fit in with the director's overall concept, but one in which the director treats his actors, not as artists to be led and nourished and shown what they can do, but as puppets to be shoved around and given meaningless bits of business to perform. Acting? Come on, let's get on with the show.

So whose contemporary is Shakespeare? From Bogdanov's production a bizarre, witless but energetic hack emerges, someone who might imagine for himself a career writing sit-coms but still needs to learn how to get his storyline right. He is neither a Renaissance lyric poet nor a modern populist, lacking both the complex imagination of the one and the manipulative skills of the other. Bogdanov presents a non-Shakespeare, a packaged product with nothing inside; and as long as the poor old Arts

Council doggedly supports such work, coachloads after coachloads of kids will sit through such tedious tosh and imagine that
they have seen Shakespeare. It's a mad world, my masters. End
of story.

When I wrote my reply, Peter became very upset and refused to
let the *Sunday Times* print it. It's okay for him to be derogatory
and insulting about theatre practitioners and their work but, in
common with most of the breed, he is surprised and hurt when
the practitioners hit back.

My reply.
An Open Letter to John Peter:

Dear John Peter,

The time is 1972. The production is Measure for Measure. (NB
– not mine) You write – 'The worst thing about Measure for
Measure . . . is its dogged insistence to be contemporary'.

Fifteen years go by. There are violent upheavals in British
society. Union busting and money madness are the order of the
day. Not for centuries has the country been so divided nor
Westminster rule so powerful. I attempt to reflect this in Henry IV
Parts 1 and 2 and Henry V. You write – 'Behind his (Bogdanov's)
determination to be 'modern' and 'relevant' there lurks a simple
minded, showbiz anxiety that the kids won't like it. Hence the
dogged attempts to be contemporary'.

A year later you are at it again. Of the Wars of the Roses,
Shakespeare's complete History Cycle you write –

'One version of Shakespeare that I feel uneasy about is what
I call The People's Shakespeare'. This is where Bogdanov's work
raises my hackles. Behind the People's Shakespeare lies the
apparent assumption that the old boy's stuff is powerful all right,
but swathed in the mist of Elizabethan history and needs to be
demystified'.

1990. Events in the country are becoming pretty cataclysmic.
You write of Coriolanus and The Winter's Tale – '. . . this is

Shakespeare for the people, which usually means that the director trusts neither Shakespeare nor the people . . . the result is a mess, pretentious but dull and politically naïve'.

21 years later. You have come of age Mr Peter. And what a birthday treat.

You are going to see Michael Bogdanov's (5th) production of Romeo and Juliet. You write –

'The trouble with Michael Bogdanov's productions . . . is that it is hell bent on making Shakespeare contemporary . . . wheezing desperately under the strain of topicality . . . impoverishes and vulgarises Shakespeare by pushing and shoving him into the 20th century'.

What does this say about both of us? That neither of us has changed in 21 years? With this one great exception. I have consistently tried, through the medium of live, as opposed to literary theatre (unlike you), to make people aware of the great issues raised in the plays with a passion and commitment born of a love of the English language. Unlike you, I have taken on board the changes in our society and have consistently been sensitive to new critical thinking – New Historicism, Cultural Materialism etc.,. At the same time I have been confronted constantly with evidence through extensive work in and for the larger community (including the founding of 7 educational groups) and having put three children through the state education system, that Shakespeare has been hi-jacked by a literary and cultural elite, of which you are a honorary member, in order to shore up its own position and to ensure the continuation in the arts of a conservative status-quo.

A few more patronising past Peterisms from the Thatcher bag. 1988. 'If you want revolutionary upheaval in order to eliminate inequality and injustice why do you feel betrayed if they are eliminated for you without upheaval?'

Oh good, John, that's all right then, I'm glad everybody's equal now.

'What's wrong with looking up words in a dictionary?' you ask.

Nothing – provided a) that you can read, b) that you possess a dictionary, and c) that you have such an intelligently retentive memory after a visit to a Shakespeare play that you can't wait to run home and investigate those 500 funny words that you can't pronounce and didn't understand. Peter and Patten – a great late 20th century double act. . .

What emerges from a review of your work over a period of time is a picture of a dangerous reactionary in whose hands a critical column is used to lambast any artist who dares to raise the flag of cultural and political dissent, a sentiment which you, being an exile from the political turmoil of Hungary in the 50's, believe is yours alone to possess. But when you write '. . . as long as the poor old Arts Council supports such work . . . it's a mad world, my masters . . .' you are dangerously close to the sentiments of the regime you left behind which would censure what it didn't believe in and eliminate what it didn't like. You are holding hands with the philistines and chauvinists who continually bleat 'I'm a taxpayer and I don't want my money wasted on that rubbish'.

Now, I make no claims for my production of Romeo and Juliet but, as it happens, others do. Some, like you, dislike it intensely, others (of whom there are many in print) think it the best version they have seen. I am quite happy to occupy the middle ground on this. But whereas in six months my production has probably reached 100,000 people, at a stroke your column has reached a potential million. Who proves to be the greater threat to our society? Me with my 'user-friendly tosh', which stands or falls by whether people wish to see it or not, or you, with your apoplectic upholding of ideologically repugnant values? As there appears to have been no change in your attitude to my work (or that of similar writers and directors) over the past 21 years, I suggest that you move over and give somebody younger a go. He/she may not like us either, but at least it would spare us the endless banality of your right-wing tub-thumping.

Michael Bogdanov

P.S. Romeo and Juliet is not a play about 'Young people being doomed by hostile fate'. The 'kids' die because they are victims of an adult world of greed and selfishness. The events which lead to their deaths are the result of a series of man-made decisions all of which could have been avoided. It is a play about existential choice and social irresponsibility, something you possess in abundance. As for the verse speaking – at a recent 'Royal' production (praised by you) I counted over 100 wrong emphases in the first hour and then gave up. At the last viewing of Romeo and Juliet I counted 25 and was horrified that so many had crept in. Is it my fault that you don't know your iambic from your pentameter?

This was not the first time I had clashed with John Peter.

* * *

For my preparation of *The Henrys*, I had looked again at the masterly Orson Welles portrayal for Falstaff in *Chimes at Midnight*. I think the version one of the best Shakespeare films ever made. Welles edits the two parts of *Henry IV* together, takes some of the dialogue and ideas from Henry V, then reshuffles text and story to come up with some extraordinary insights into the character. The film smells of sweat, dirt and war in a way I was never able to capture on stage, and which Branagh's version doesn't get anywhere near. (I started on too jokey a level with Falstaff's recruiting scene in *Henry IV Part II*, and was never able to pull it back.)

One link in particular I seized on. Welles reverses the two parts of the last scene of *Henry IV Part I* to leave Hal still at odds with his father. The King patently believes Falstaff has killed Hotspur and that Hal's claim to have done so is a lie. Obvious. And brilliant. Shakespeare finished with an apparent reconciliation between father and son at the end of Part I. But then, at the beginning of Part 2, they are estranged again, although it is only shortly after the Battle of Shrewsbury. The problem is that he wrote the second part some time after the first.

It is possible, though unlikely, that (a) on completing Part 1 he didn't know he would write Part 2 and (b) taking Part 1 complete in itself, the story had to have a resolution. For us, Part 2 following Part 1 on Saturdays one hour later, the effect of finishing Part 1 with this reversal was electric. It left the story wide open, with the audience buzzing with excitement to know what followed. It involved no text alterations. Many a member of the audience came back in the afternoon to find out how the story resolved itself, and then couldn't resist staying for the evening as well. (Stories of baby-sitting rows, spouses refusing to leave cars behind, emergency arrangements to get home – or stay the night – filtered back every week.) Of course, there were always the silly ones who couldn't bear the reversed ending. As if it matters. And they should be so lucky to know the text in the first place.

Thus John Peter in *The Sunday Times*. Apart from finding some of the comic business 'coarse beyond belief' and that I suffer from 'dogged attempts' to be 'contemporary' and that 'This sort of rabble-rousing rubbish distorts and vulgarises Shakespeare's cool tough line on power politics', he concludes that I feel that Shakespeare needs my helping hand: 'he switches round the last two scenes of Part 1 for the sake of what he fondly imagines is a psychological insight'. No John, Orson Welles' insight.

John Peter is Hungarian. The problem with being an exile in love with Shakespeare is that one becomes more traditional than the traditionalists. Irving Wardle asserts that 'John Peter has every right to rend English playwrights limb from limb for their flirtations with Marxism; not because this viewpoint happens to coincide with that of *The Sunday Times* and its readers, but because, as a Hungarian émigré who witnessed the 1956 Russian invasion, he knows more about the realities of Marxism than the 'state of Britain' authors, whose interest in revolutionary politics has yet to come between them and a hot dinner'.

Apart from anything else, this runs completely counter to an argument earlier in Wardle's book, where he declares that experience isn't everything. I accept there is nothing worse than amateur dabblers in the field of politics in art, however, if the 'you weren't there, so you can't write about it' brigade were to be correct, the world would have been deprived of a thousand masterpieces. I find John Peter's belief that he has a patent on middle-European thinking and politics hard to stomach, particularly as he left when the going got rough. There are many of us who have close acquaintance with exile, the holocaust, torture, totalitarianism and atrocities and I find it offensive to be lectured to on the level of a ten year old school boy. And even if this were not the case, an argument akin to 'I'm older than you so I must know better' never cuts much ice. I have relatives who died in the pogroms and concentration camps, but I don't consider that I have a right to express myself on these matters over and above others who feel as strongly as I do about human rights, but who have never had anything more harassing happen to them than a run in with a parking meter.

I am often asked which critic I dislike most. I find myself hard pushed. There are many contenders and, although it sounds as though John Peter is my *bete noire* among English critics, he isn't.

No, the Prince of Prats for my money – and I earn a bob or two these days despite the efforts of the above, is totally unpredictable, he appears to have no criteria by which he operates, is whimsical, subjective, dependent on whom he's with, whether he's eaten, where his seat is, whether it's raining, if he's got a cold. He is a vicious, nasty, vituperative, vitriolic, objectionable, abusive, arrogant, excretory, disgruntled, cavilling, sniping (I've got the Thesaurus in front of me), small-minded, petty, carping, quibbling, arse-licking, bum-sucking, toadying, sycophant, who should never be let near a theatre again.

One day I'll say what I really think.

Bibliography

Recycling Shakespeare, Charles Marowitz, Palgrave Macmillan 1991

Theatre Criticism, Irving Wardle, Routledge 1992

Shakespeare Our Contemporary, Jan Kott, Methuen 1964

The Wars of the Roses, Michael Pennington and Michael Bogdanov, Nick Hern Books

Politics and Poetics of Transgression, Stallybrass and White, Routledge, 1986

William Shakespeare, Terry Eagleton, Basil Blackwell, 1986

Chekov A Biography, Benedetti, Stanislavsky, Methuen 1988

The Work, Wealth and Happiness of Mankind H.G. Wells, Doubleday, Doran and Company, 1931

Shakespeare
The Director's Cut
by Michael Bogdanov

The new edition of Michael's book of essays is a combination of Volumes 1 and 2 and four new essays on *Othello, Twelfth Night, A Midsummer Night's Dream* and *As You Like It* so that essays on the tragedies, histories and comedies are all covered in one volume.

> . . . boy did I enjoy the riffs on the plays. These are not production nor performance notes, and certainly not academic analyses, but rather – what is this play about? Why was it written (other than an urgent need to put paying bums on benches by next Thursday?) He storms us with a blizzard of ideas, more than could ever be used in any lifetime's stagings.
>
> *The Guardian*

DOP: 08 August 2013
ISBN: 978-1-909305-31-1
Price: £9.99

www.capercailliebooks.co.uk

Capercaillie Books